BARBWIRE NOOSE ®

FEAR IS THE ROOT OF ALL WEAKNESS ©

MAKE WORLDS

Fear Is The Root of All Weakness®

Marcia Anita Hobbs MARCIA BNOOSE

ANYTHING BUT ORDINARY

Judgement and Perception have NO value here.©

AUTOBIOGRAPHICAL SERIES

BARBWIRE NOOSE
FEAR IS THE ROOT OF ALL WEAKNESS

iv

ABOUT THE AUTHOR

Human Rights Activist Marcia BNoose.

Author, born as Marcia Anita Hobbs in Rose Park, Adelaide, South Australia, 25th April 1984.

In 2015, Le Droit Humain Co-Freemasonry, Lodge 406.

When the most Honest thing you can ever say is the Oddest thing you will ever say… "I wouldn't change a day or have it any other way." – Marcia Anita Hobbs, aka Marcia

BNoose, "Anything But Ordinary." – Judgment and Perception Have No Value Here; Autobiographical Series.

The content of this is Real. Candid, clumsy, courageous, and curious. Enjoy x

DEDICATION

To everyone I love and to Justice for All.

For everyone who believes in the Universal Declaration of Human Rights, shall Good always prevail over evil.

Contents

A Better World. To Justice for All. Truth Matters.

This Series of Books.

Autobiographies, A Brand Dedicated To 'A Better World' – Human Rights. The Autobiographical Series 'Anything But Ordinary – Judgement And Perception Have No Value Here' is a collection of books full of candid facts, Experiences, Quotes, and open to Interpretation, depending on where the Reader's head is at – Judgment, Education, My Life, And Thoughts. Stories Of The Heart, Mind, and Soul, Consisting Of Personal Views, knowledge, and life experiences, as well as light- hearted, Comedic References, Poetry, World facts, and More.

Quoting A Letter To Professor Fatima Meer From The Book

'Conversations With Myself' By Nelson Mandela: "The Trouble, Of Course, Is That Most Successful Men Are Prone To Some Form Of Vanity. There Comes A Stage In Their Lives When They Consider It Permissible To Be Egotistic And To Brag To The Public At Large About Their Unique Achievements. What a Sweet Euphemism for Self-Praise the English Language Has Evolved! Autobiography, They Choose To Call It, Where The Shortcomings Of Others Are Frequently Exploited To Highlight The Praiseworthy

Accomplishments Of The Author."

As a true crime writer and author of biographical literature, I Could Relate To Nelson Mandela's View of Autobiography. Though I Have Made Sure My Life's Evolution In Its Imperfections And Perfections has been Equally Shared, I cannot Help But Feel At Times The Personalness Of My autobiographies has truthfully And Graphically Shared the Shortcomings Of Others, Not Just My Own. Being Mindful Not To Brag Yet Proud Of My Achievements, This Euphemism Interpretation Is Bang On The Realities Of A Biographical Record. The Highs And The Lows Of Life, Often Shared Moments. When The Hunter Talks Of Killing The Lion, It Is The Hunter's Life That Is Glorified, Though The Lion Has Great Achievements Of Its Own Unshared, As A Hunter Only KnowS His Own Life And The Lion's Role In It.

Human Rights Matter

Anything But Ordinary –

Judgment and Perception have

NO

VALUE HERE.

Book No. 1

(of however many books in the series I would like)

CHAPTERS

ONE - YOUTH to 30's - TRAUMA IN A NUTSHELL

With the bra size of the wondrous 10DD came the responsibility of illegally, irregularly, buying alcohol at 16 and a half for myself and friends. Youth underaged drinking in regional South Australia, with and without parental supervision, was not uncommon.

I'll start by clarifying that I didn't party half as much as

gossip has it.

TWO - COUNTRY TO CITY LIVING

Country living is laidback compared to city living – you get to smell the roses.

THREE - A LIFE OF ENDLESS LIVES

One Testing Experience Too Many. A Life of Endless Lives and A Yellow Curtain Blind.

FOUR - TEACHING

Aquatics Teaching as a teenager forced me to grow up quickly; if you wanted to keep your job in a small town, you needed to act responsibly. The older sister in my family, I was used to responsibility. Often taking the mature role around the house, I was already very sensible. Teaching enhances that sense of responsibility and grooms you into a person (if you wish or care) with respectable public conduct, considering the watchful judgment of others.

FIVE - LOVER TO LOVER

"No one is born hating another person because of the colour of his skin, or his background, or his religion. People must learn to hate, and if they can learn to hate, they can be taught to love, for love comes more naturally to the human heart than its opposite."

- Nelson Mandela, Long Walk to Freedom.

SIX - VICPOL AND DAME PHYLLIS FROST CENTRE

I recorded every request I made; every request was ignored. A dot-point daily diary of the hours and interactions I had with staff behind the DPFC's dirty walls. Requests for hay fever tablets were denied, access to my asthma puffer was denied, and access to basic property provided to other inmates was denied.

SEVEN - POETRY

Poems by yours truly.

EIGHT - STUDY

Never Stop Learning. No one knows everything, and you never know enough.

NINE - VOLUNTEERING

The most significant achievements I have made in life have not been on a payroll.

TEN - FREEMASONRY

"The source of every crime is some defect of the understanding, or some error in reasoning, or some sudden force of the passions. Defect in the understanding is ignorance; in reasoning, erroneous opinion." - Thomas Hobbes, Leviathan.

ELEVEN - OPINIONS AND RANDOM SHIT

Opinions are like assholes, everyone's got one - these are mine. Plus, Anything but Ordinary random shit.

Chapter One

'Youth ages into my thirties – Trauma in a Nutshell'

What has been written about a lot is the trauma, the drama, and the corruption. Both Autobiographies, The Story Behind the Brand BARBWIRE NOOSE and UGLY HEROS The Price of Unlawful Enforcement account for the turmoil caused in government cover ups more than anything else. This series of books, with its autobiographical content, I hope, is a little more light-hearted, like me, happy-go-lucky. Though some chapters outline the serious impact whistleblowing has had on my life and survival, this ongoing series of books is more focused on the beauty and stupidity of life.

I've always been a poet, complimented by both my English teacher and drama teacher for my literature during high school. I take great joy in the fact that, in my thirties, I've had the opportunity to share sweet nothings, sorrow, and touching poems with the world. Here's one, more to come.

DEFINE LOVE

If I had to choose between the stars and the sky, I would choose the sky and hold you forever. – Marcia Anita Hobbs 30/11/2018 (and that's precisely what I did, my moon, I love you xo)

My passions are numerous, and consistency can be an illusion in my life at times. Universally driven, I believe I have spent most of my days blessed by all the greatest energies our universe holds. Quantum Physics - spectroscopy, study of the absorption and emission of light and

other radiation by matter, as related to the dependence of these processes on the wavelength of the radiation; as defined by Britannica. We are Matter. Escalating into a science lesson rather quickly here. Quantum physics is a topic for a deeper discussion in another book.

Passionate about literature and historical learning –

without being a walking encyclopedia. My interests from Britannica are something I share with you in these books, current facts, and stuff.

I enjoy books, antiques, unique experiences, and typically the finer things in life. A clean environment, good food, and good company are always complementary to a satisfying standard of living.

I lived very privately in my twenties, for ten years of my life, allowing only a handful of people into my home. My home was my refuge, with the backyard my two dogs' sanctuary. A German Shepard and also a Kelpie/King Charles Spaniel/Jack Russell mix. Living like royalty in my home, I needed nor wanted for much, living in the abundance of my desires.

I grew up absolutely loving horses and horse riding, and I still do. I grew up with horses and actually used to sketch them. Sketching - an arts and crafts activity as enjoyable as looking after and raising animals.

I'm a great shot with a bow and arrow. Rating myself behind a gun barrel, too – I'm better than most local cops (yes, that's a dig). Some would say that's not a hard achievement, and I would agree. Either way, I'm a damn good shot. During my teenage years spent on a farm, we had our own motorbike track with jumps, and I had been riding a motorbike since I was eight years old. Dad made us a go-kart with a 125cc motorbike motor, three gears, and a roll cage.

Driving and steering have been a way of life for much of my life. I would go drifting in a roll-caged Datsun out in the pines after getting my P plates and have actually undergone a defensive driving course – not by choice, but I was stoked it happened. Read 'The Story Behind the Brand BARBWIRE NOOSE' for a little more on that.

I've indulged in skydiving (tandem at this stage), steered a small airplane, and can whistle with an acorn top.

Other stuff about me is that since my early teens, I've been able to snowboard, rock climb, mountain bike, kick the footy, been a boxing enthusiast, danced around the house, and sung my lungs out. You thought we were listening to sport, didn't you? Not quite, I didn't actually like Physical education much in high school. I love watching sports, and I think I'd play tennis or stick to my extreme sports indulgence if anything. Love a treadmill, but hate the gym scene – that's me.

On singing, I think I'm okay at it. In high school, I was chosen to sing the solo part in a school event, where we sang 'Time After Time' by Cyndi Lauper.

Fashion was a passion as a teen, more alterations than from scratch tailoring. I had some staple brand- named clothes and a closet mainly filled with Adelaide fashion, as all my relatives lived in South Australia's Capital, around five hundred kilometers from Mount Gambier.

Home life was strict but happy. My stoner parents were generally happy, family life at home had a few dramas and quirks like all families, yet was mainly great and grounded.

In High School, to start with, I wanted to be a veterinarian or a psychologist. I did my first year's work experience at the Vet. They put down so many animals that week, I was put off that job for life. Instead, I chose to successfully pursue my passion to study Law at University (entry 2001, deferred start for 2002) after this experience. Work experience the following year was much more enjoyable. Not opting for what I was planning to contribute to society in slave labor - jokes, I decided to pursue a more satisfying work experience opportunity the following year – paintball. No joke. It was so fun! I spent a week shooting paintball guns and checking out paintball ranges. One of my peers, who failed to get work experience and liked my idea, joined me, which was cool.

Adolescence with the bra size of the wondrous 10DD came with the responsibility of illegally irregularly buying alcohol at 16 and a half for myself and friends. Youth underaged drinking in regional South Australia, with and without parental supervision, was not uncommon.

I'll start by clarifying that I didn't party half as much as gossip has it. After being sexually assaulted by what to me was an old man. Around my dad's age (a further traumatic fact about it all), a predatory SAPOL police officer, sworn to serve and protect, not prey on young, vulnerable girls.

I, one of many young women, was vulnerable prey to Kurt Gavan Slaven (DOB 07NOV1958). My recovery involved medicating my PTSD with medicinal cannabis, going out with my mates and drinking at the local pubs and nightclubs, for about 6 months straight. I had a boyfriend, one year older than me. Most of my mates were basically a year older than me (1983 babies, myself a 1984 child), and I was one of the younger members of the classroom during high school. Going out and having fun on Thursday, Friday, and Saturday nights drowned the sexual abuse trauma caused by now-retired SAPOL criminal cop Kurt Gavan Slaven, whose retirement came in 2018 after I made a statement against him for his sex crimes. In 2001, I dyed my hair blonde after the sexual assault – cognitive dissociation did the rest. Dissociation is a mental process of disconnecting from one's thoughts, feelings, memories, or sense of identity.

Back in the day, if you were under eighteen years of age, you could stay in pubs until quite late, and showing identification (ID) was not compulsory. By the time we all left school, we'd all already been in pubs locally and consumed alcohol. I had a good, mainly sensible bunch of friends. We looked out for each other when we were out and having fun, fun that made me feel normal after suffering a sex crime classed as paedophilia, against a minor under seventeen years of age in South Australia. Turning eighteen years old approximately six months plus after most of my mates, my inherited adult anatomy (those DD's, my Mother's anatomy – her figure stunning during most of her life) allowed me to stay in pubs and clubs after midnight under the age of eighteen, coupled with a fake ID, it was basically assured that I could hang out with my mates and party until close time.

I was never too irresponsible (I don't think). It's easy to misconstrue the past, especially when mobile phones were not walking cameras.

When I reported in 2014, the SAPOL officer who committed a sex crime against me at sixteen years old – Kurt Gavan Slaven (DOB 07NOV1958), I NEVER expected a cover-up. The offense committed in 2001, before my seventeenth Birthday. An offence committed while Officer Kurt Slaven was on duty, assigned to investigate the theft of my car. A VH Commodore vehicle, which had been in a vehicle collision the day before the theft. Upon finalising the report, before SAPOL taking a formal statement, I experienced firsthand the devastating impact of family siding with a perpetrator—a common occurrence in sex offence cases, and a shocking fact to many, including myself. I choose not to talk to my family unless I want to, due to this

14

fact and many other sour and inhumane lows they hit during a decade of whistleblowing. The victim blaming, seedy cover-up, and intentional malicious activity caused me devastating emotional distress and lifelong psychological trauma. On my mother's side of the family, I don't actually understand why they sided with the offender, seemingly consistent narcissistic behaviour like denying my Aunties' cries of molestation by an uncle. Greed, pride, and power are all I see behind this type of callousness, every time. At this time in life, my cousin was marrying a SAPOL officer's son, and my cousin was a SAPOL officer – these were the interests protected over my credibility, justice, and justice for people with disabilities. The reactions of my Nanna's and family to my report to SAPOL regarding the police officer were dismissive, condescending, and bizarre to me. None of my poppas were alive to add reason to rumour, I was surrounded by mainly pretentious women role models and typical dominating, proud men.

STANLEY HOBBS

Stanley Hobbs

The previous responses to domestic violence, sexual violence revelations, including incestuous acts, clearly repeat because of the family's ignorance and the use of ostracism. I failed to understand their dehumanisation but was not surprised. It takes some planning to surprise me these days. My Father's side of the family, consisting of SAPOL and ex-SAPOL members, it was easy to understand their dehumanising position to choose pride and profession over the truth. Though equally disappointing and rift-creating, I have no respect for either side of my family's decisions. Both families ostracized me and even blamed me for ruining the offender's lives. Victim blaming with comments of promiscuity, untrue, and small-minded. Shameful reactions to which I find unforgivable. The following acceptable scapegoat perceptions shine a light on the sadly typical victim-blaming to which many survivors endure.

My family is dysfunctional, both my mother's and my father's side. Full of secrets they cover up with pride, characterized by dismissive behavior - including gaslighting, finger-pointing, and blatant lies. What followed was a deeper character assassination, truth-distorting agendas, and gas lighting/domestic abuse and narcissistic saga. This statement from research summing up the truth of dysfunction related to sex offending, relatively well, Living with the emotional effects of sexual abuse is painful enough. Unfortunately, many survivors open up about their abuse only to find that their family members' reactions toward them are just as painful

— if not more so — than the original trauma. It may shock some people to learn that family members often choose to side with sexual abuse perpetrators and against their victims, especially if the abuse was committed within the family. The truths shared by sexual abuse survivors are consistent in the myriad of ways that their families scold and reject them in the aftermath of disclosure, all while favouring their abusers. The brave survivor gets left out of family gatherings; if the abuse is inside the family, the abusers are often invited over to the victim. Many victims are pressured to "forgive" the perpetrator (justification of the abuse) and even to consider the abuser's feelings, even while the victim's own trauma and responses toward the perpetrator are overlooked, condoning the abuser and condemning the victim. After reporting abuse, the pride of the family dominates to victimise the victim further. A Survivor pressing charges against their perpetrators often ends up ostracised and blamed for ruining the abuser's life, despite the apparent hypocrisy of this statement. In these situations, perpetrators are embraced and favoured by family members as they join together in shutting down acknowledgment of, or attention to, sexual abuse. Survivors, on the other hand, are blamed and viewed as the troublemakers in the family.

I believe there is no more genuine sorrow than the loss of the love between a child and a parent. I know this, feel this, live this.

Forgiveness is a privilege, not a virtue.

Quickly going into generational sex offences, and the reaction of my Indian mother's family, who migrated to Australia before my mum was born, a few of her siblings were born in India. The family (Indian Royalty descendants) has two (2) sex offenders in it, that I directly know of. Two (2) sex offenders who committed sex offences against family members, and two (2) sex offenders who were broadly ignored by the family and invited to family gatherings despite the crimes they had committed against other family members. My Mother shared Birthday gatherings with a creep. I grew up believing this creep was jailed and released when I was a teen. If my Mother's Indian Family had it their way, he probably never would have seen jail at all. My

18

Mother's sister was sexually abused by her uncle as a child (young teenager), and I believe he has never been charged. My aunt's claims were dismissed, and the family often labels her as having troublemaking tendencies.

Unfortunately, a survivor of more sexual abuse than I would wish on an enemy – myself, never wishing sexual violations upon any soul. I know too well there are no words to alleviate the pain; you can be an ear and have much respect for all survivors and their stories alike. Sex crimes are not only vile but life- devastating. I wish all rape victims peace, justice, and strength, along with capital punishment for their offenders, which is not a thing in the Australian justice system – a bittersweet fact of life.

The least that can be done, I think, to stop sexual abuse is the police acting responsibly, charges being laid, victims being believed, and the names of sex offenders NEVER suppressed. I think there are more grounds to suppress the name of a murderer than there will ever be to suppress the name of a sex offender.

Back to some light-heartedness. Live music, my most faithful love, I've got a collection of memorabilia and have licked the guitar pick from the mouth of the lead singer from the metal band Sevendust. Proud moment. A conversation with Danny Carey, drummer in the TOOL band, was another highlight of my late twenties. I've had so many Fuck Yes moments in life that the bad things, though hard, have

never overshadowed them. Good memories, and even some of my
not-so-fine hours, have been spent with music.

A photo from 2004 of me smoking a joint (marijuana treats my PTSD - I am personally against pharmaceutical treatment, all natural is the way for me as much as possible) at the Big Day Out (BDO) music Festival in Adelaide immortalises the best of the worst of bulimia and anorexia.

I was borderline anorexic at eighteen years of age. I spent seventeen years of my life bulimic; it wasn't until my 30s that I developed healthier eating habits. The BDO Jack Daniels photographer also captured my wallet chain size and waistline. A photo of myself and a fellow music festival fan who had a Jack Daniel's singlet on this fine BDO day – an image we could download via a link the photographer provided. When I say wallet chain waist, I'm being literal (note I'm basically five feet tall). I bought a wallet chain from a stall, which I wore as a belt that day. I recall vividly arguing with the salesman as I told him I was buying the bike chain wallet chain to wear as my belt. He assured me this chain, which I cherished for over fifteen years, was not going to clip up around my waist, saying it was too small for anyone to wear as a belt. I bought it and clipped it up right in front of him. His shock – his disgust was blatantly obvious. The problem was, I couldn't see how skinny I was in the mirror.

Body confidence is important. Self-confidence is more important. Healthy living, being authentic to yourself, and being faithful to the truth are all essential virtues.

Entering my twenties, buying a house at twenty-one opened and closed a lot of doors in my life. I could crank my stereo at full volume, and no one complained or seemed to care. Beautifying the yard, which had roses, I established a cactus garden. I am a hopeless gardener; I don't water my plants, then wonder briefly why they died. Always a bit anti-social, I loved having my own place with no inspections, pets, and a private backyard. In my own home, I could use the same reason as everyone else to hibernate, outside of attending special occasions - the old 'home loan financial strain'

excuse. Even though I was always paying extra on my loan, I was well ahead in payments. It felt like a further freedom buying a home, the feeling I felt when I obtained my car licence. An affordable home loan allowed for more travel to Adelaide events and trips, as well as trips from Mount Gambier to Melbourne to shop. It was also the door to long-term bulimia nervosa, my own space to regurgitate sugary delights and everything else I consumed. I traveled extensively to attend heavy metal concerts, big-name shows, and festivals. Seeing a large portion of music that I'm a mega fan of. My twenties were a very happy, satisfying time of life. Living and hustling, building my dreams, my brand – Barbwire Noose.

To earn my crust to live like a little rock princess, buy shoes, designer sunglasses, brand threads, do my nails, and have what I think are the best cosmetics at the time. I was mostly a swim teacher during the days and in the afternoons for nearly two decades. I am also a half-qualified Real Estate agent – I hated it, so fuck finishing the course.

Life was simple and I was humble – for the most part. I like to think I still am humble.

My thirties saw me publicly promote myself a bit and participate in pageantry events, traveling to Jamaica and the USA in 2018 to represent Australia. It's great to get dressed up, but to me, it was a scene of ego and some nasty backstage behavior, and that wasn't worth the effort. To me, the second most considerable appeal of pageantry is having an excuse to dress up. The first appeal is to showcase and influence charity and volunteering. The reality is that you can get dressed up for no reason at all and go out to dinner, which costs the same or less, plus someone else does the dishes.

You may have seen me on television, starring as an extra in numerous television series, commercials, pageants, and modeling campaigns for my brand, Barbwire Noose ®.

I finished off my thirties using OnlyFans to prove the defamation police and creepy criminals ignited about me being a prostitute (I have NEVER been a sex worker!) was out of control. OnlyFans had been an excellent platform for me after the trauma of Endless strip searches in extradition and incarceration. Until they told me I wasn't me, I couldn't consent to my content, or I was underage. None of these were applicable, and at the time of this publication, the reason for one of these was unfounded. Redeeming a little control over how people see my (bluntly put) cunt, especially as a sexual crime survivor, has helped in the recovery of some of my self-worth, self- confidence, and dignity.

That said, judge me if you wish, don't count on me caring about your opinion.

Life as a young adult was mainly work. After work, I would chill in the evenings with my dogs and boyfriend, watching TV, listening to music, indulging hobbies - primarily crafting things and smoking weed. Going to the gym, engaging in personal training, walking around the Blue Lake, and exploring the gorgeous town of Mount Gambier were my regular habits.

On the drearier days of winter, I would indulge in the little luxuries of my home and pamper myself somewhat. I actually hate the word pamper and would much rather call it self-care, indulging in face masks, manicures, hair treatments, gourmet cooking, sewing/design, and loud music on my own in the house, the majority of the time.

Suppose the budget was entirely spent on Barbwire Noose or travel, materialism, or self-care. In that case, I'd sit, listening to music, watching TV, or scouring the internet for acting and modeling opportunities. Madly in love with the story of King Arthur, I'm a massive fan of watching Merlin. My other television crushes include ABC's 24/7 news, The Nanny, Friends, daytime soaps, and documentaries, which I occasionally plan my daytime routines around to watch. My current favourite go-to movies are the SAW horror movie series or DC/Marvel, like Deadpool. These will change, so I'll update you in the next volume. YouTube is cool to learn real shit and bullshit, like TV, so I indulge that too.

Farm life with my parents and the simple life I led for a decade changed so dramatically as I became a globally known fashion designer, corporate brand owner, and public human rights activist in my thirties. The limestone coast area is a delight that you only truly appreciate when you move away.

"You live but once this lifetime – be uniquely and fiercely you in everything you do. Let your positive light shine and NEVER stray from your TRUTH no matter what life brings you." – Marcia Anita Hobbs (BNoose).

Chapter Two

'Country to City Living'

Country living is laidback compared to city living – you get to smell the roses.

I moved to the Capital city of South Australia, Adelaide, in 2021 out of necessity. Whistleblowing had become hectic; it seemed that everyone had skeletons in their closet, and most cared not for the truth, justice, or people with disabilities, but only for themselves.

Before reporting sex offender Kurt Gavan Slaven, and a cover-up plot to blame another SAPOL sex offender, Andrew Cherry, my life had been severely endangered after assisting the police force with the murder of a drug addict who would have never seen justice without my speaking up for him. Plus, the rest of the police and governance malfeasance. Abhorrent criminal negligence from numerous Australian police forces nationally, following 2014, SAPOL was involved in severe institutional abuse, misconduct, and criminality against my person, which spanned over a decade.

Police and defence force personnel, as well as political ministers guilty of conspiracy in efforts to achieve a cover-up of sex crimes, persons are guilty of an offence that occurs when two or more people agree to commit an unlawful act or to achieve a lawful goal through unlawful means, with the intention to carry out the agreement. Key elements include a mutual "meeting of minds" (agreement) and the intention to commit the unlawful act. The offence is complete upon the agreement itself and is considered an inchoate or preparatory crime. Elements of Conspiracy:

For a conviction, the prosecution must prove these elements beyond a reasonable doubt:

1. Agreement: A formal or informal agreement exists between two or more people to pursue a common, unlawful objective.

2. Unlawful Purpose: The agreed-upon objective is either an illegal act or a legal act carried out through illegal means.

3. Intention: The conspirators must have a genuine intent to carry out the unlawful act or pursue the unlawful purpose, not just discuss it.

Discussing efforts to conflate and confuse the investigation involving a character assassination used to discard lives by a corrupt police culture, often referring to drug addiction as a reason to discriminate against a victim. Furthermore, lending thought to avenues of 'guilty by association'.

The approach of dehumanising to discriminate is evident throughout the ages, especially in the inequality between the white and black races.

Dehumanisation seeded by perception and the police force influences the views of the community, allowing many persons to go unaccountable for sex offences (especially against sex workers) and murder in drug-related crimes, and this should not be the case. Unjust and intentional outcomes are sorted by all involved and many around them. What I personally witnessed regarding the dehumanisation of a drug addict was some justice for the victim, but not really – the instigator of the murder avoiding charges at the time and causing much more destruction to the regional area as he continued to try to be a Kingpin of, as well as consuming, Ice/Methamphetamines. After getting away with ordering the victim to be 'dealt with', Tim Stringer, a full-blown drug addict himself who played informant even though he was the main reason the murder occurred - the instigator between Tim and his friend Shaun MacDonnell whose needs for ICE had them chase a position of dealing, mainly to people who could not afford it resulting in them owing for the debts. Payments to these wannabes for debts included favours, stolen goods, serious acts of crime, including assault, extortion, murder, domestic violence, etc.

The homicide investigation was engaged during a SAPOL investigation into the sex industry, which led to a police cover-up of their use of prostitutes (including children) and sex crimes. My knowledge regarding these investigations came from my assistance with the homicide investigation. Because of years of severe criminal negligence by police, and also these men's criminality, this was, in the end, the basis of the many reasons I was forced to move to the city—the efforts to character-assassinate and distort investigations surrounding me. Labelled a crown witness in 2022 by authorities, which could only have come about during the years of the homicide investigation, was outstanding. The move from country to city living further exposed that SAPOL and other state plus federal police forces had irrefutable agendas to induce and encourage sex crimes to be committed against me. I was being intentionally targeted by persons known to police, malicious criminal negligence by SAPOL, due to my knowing about their criminal conduct, because I knew of and was reporting their vile sex crimes and cover-up.

Malicious intentional torts causing bodily harm, and reckless actions of criminal negligence by police, escalating out of control as they desperately tried to ignore me and keep the truth out of the media. Channel ten (and NT News) is proving they very much supported the suppression of the facts, not wanting to be contacted regarding the Autobiographical, irrefutable, and plainly put - the transparent truth. Personally, I am unsurprised by Channel 10's desire to control what is in the public interest; at this time, hosts were leaving the network in droves. At the same time, the channel lost a significant number of viewers – how would they get ahead without metaphorically speaking sucking corrupt elite dicks, including the government? As if they were going to rock any boats in their ongoing campaign to save has-been TV programs. Channel 10 in 2024 failed to follow through with the Barbwire Noose® 'Human Rights Matter' Television Commercial airing – the network's ignorance towards me and Human Rights is blatantly apparent, and admittedly feels personal. Journalists of this time (2015 – 2025) should have been ashamed of their efforts to flounder in publishing the truth to the public.

I witnessed so much malfeasance and criminality at the taxpayers' expense. Police Ministers evidently approved an endless misappropriation of taxpayer funds, as I wrote to them regarding departmental concerns that called for a Royal Commission into police forces (particularly SAPOL), which compromises civilians' safety and national security in a cover-up of numerous government departmental crimes. The climate of Australian governance is riddled with corruption and policing corruption under both serving governments throughout its established history. Integrity bodies established as independent have failed to address the corrupt shortcomings of ministers and funding organisations alike. The Story Behind the Brand BARBWIRE NOOSE detailing the brand's establishment stemming from my reporting of governance human rights breaches.

An established fashion label owner of over 15 years. My brand has international supply chains, billboards with me as the lead designer and model for Barbwire Noose. A US brand had selected me, as the designer behind Barbwire Noose, to showcase a six-piece collection at New York Fashion Week in September 2021. I had applied online for the opportunity in 2020 and was actually selected for the dream opportunity. Stoked, I was so excited. The most exciting times of my life and for my brand turned into a complete nightmare, plagued by the government's desperate need to discredit me.

I'm here, a force, a storm – not just some designer. My **Barbwire Noose** line, it's not just clothes; it's a statement, a 'Do NOT Conform' scream against the system. I write, I speak, I dress to empower, to tear down the walls of injustice.

A plot trying to discredit a respected member of the limestone coast, a fashion designer, Human Rights Activist, author, whistle-blower, Australian citizen, and advocate for the mute, non-cognitive disabled persons, I witnessed severe abuse in South Australia's government disability sector. Furthermore, trying to discredit a person with submissions to Royal Commission(s) and plotting to further harm and discredit a victim of police paedophilia, who had endured a gross level of defamation due to police criminal negligence, which had been endless since at least 2012. Suffering from criminal negligence by police for a decade, and most severely, was recklessly endangered since

2016. The most damage was caused by defamatory slander by police officers throughout South Australia and Victoria. The move to the city, with its large population, should have led people to be less indulgent in malicious accusations. I should have been living in a position where no one, except for corrupt police, would have been motivated negatively. Not the case. Unfortunately, after years of defamation and the police encouraged affray activities, my presence in Adelaide was no different from that of the malicious actions engaged in the small town of Mount Gambier. Police and their affray of associations with shit humans having nothing better to do than lie and believe lies about me in a cover-up of sex crimes. Bigotry and those who comply with torts and torturous activities, like with the Nazis on said enemies, is a weak state of mind I loathe with little mercy.

Regarding the defamation, facts are that I was personally first exposed to the malicious and defamatory remarks circulating about my life and brand Barbwire Noose after my dad was attacked by offenders who trespassed in 2012. I stood up for my dad at this time, writing to the media. Dad was attacked by petty drug dealers – Gypsy Joker noms. I wrote to Channel 7 News about the attack, and the reporter turned politician Frank Pangallo (DOB15OCT1954).

Frank Pangallo took an interest in the story. In my opinion, Frank Pangallo is a disappointment in both roles of responsibility:

investigative journalism and politics. His moral compass is at a level where he fails to act diligently to expose sexual assaults against the disabled, government sector paedophilia, or the depths of the police links to the ICE industry and substandard paedophile peddling and protecting bikers at the expense of the community and victims.

My approach to telling Dad's story to the media was encouraged by my Mum and Uncle, Dad's brother, with whom I believed did this with Dad's knowledge. This was not the case; Dad was not aware I had spoken to the media. Doing the right thing apparently caused a lot of drama, including the escalation of a private intimate video of me committing a sex act on my partner, filmed while drunk after a dinner at the Commodore Motel, a short walk from my property. The revenge porn that was apparently circulating in 2011 was further distributed via Silk Road. The circulation of this revenge porn caused irreparable damage to my life, over a decade of severe reckless endangerment, stalkers, sex crimes stemming from the circulated revenge porn, torts and crimes coerced by police and felons, plus an admission that police were covering up paedophilia – and were proud of it in 2020.

Witnessing all these ongoing events during a time when VICPOL declared my phone was tapped. Investigations federally approved to a level where a state I did not reside in breached the Privacy Act, and numerous states overheard and then overlooked sex offenses against me, showing a sick extent of lows the police force was willing to go to cover up sex crimes. The lack of separation of powers between the police and the judicial system is also at a paramount level of exposure. A beacon of the failure of Australia's institutions to uphold the constitution, like 'The Mullighan Inquiry'. Personally, I think an enquiry should be held into the mental state and physical life span of victims who took part in the Mullighan Inquiry. I'm sure there would be evidence of institutional abuse hindering their lives, with a misappropriation of taxpayers' funds being used for the harassment agendas. The Labor government was responsible for the suppression, with liberals just as big beneficiaries, and police sex offenders getting a free ride. The police are irrefutably determined to try to assist suicide with their relentless illegalities, creating turmoil, and these intentional efforts to cause the demise of my life. For better or worse, I am blessed as a mother fucker on a mission can be. I've survived it all, thus far. Amen.

The 2021 move to Adelaide was for nine months, and I faced many life-threatening circumstances of near homelessness, assault, harassment, and sexual assault during this period. By this stage, I honestly regretted doing the right thing. A country girl's first real experience of city living. Experiences that only added to the traumatic turmoil of what my life had become during my thirties, the apparent prime of life. Only three states were suitable for Barbwire Noose. SA, meaning Adelaide, where it had presence, Victoria -

Melbourne, where I had supply chains and presence, or New South Wales - Sydney, to really get in the thick of Australian fashion retail. I had celebrated turning thirty with my brother, who lived in Queensland. Spending a short time on the Gold Coast of the state at Burleigh Heads, I could tell it wasn't a place for me personally, or the best place to expand my brand. Perhaps New South Wales, Bondi, or just below the Gold Coast would be a better fit. Having traveled to Adelaide frequently throughout my upbringing and enjoyed the city's lifestyle on weekends, I ultimately chose to stay in Adelaide, despite my love for Chadstone shopping. Numerous influences solidified my decision in the end.

At twenty-eight years old, I had planned to move to Melbourne. I had incorporated my brand to expand Barbwire Noose further in the fashion hub of Australia. The savage criminal offence against my dad in March 2012 led to my staying in Mount Gambier.

The city of Adelaide is beautiful, also known as aka the city of churches. For my brand, it provided boutique embellishments and fabrics that were not readily available in regional parts of Australia. Perfect to tailor my designs for the New York Fashion Week opportunity presented by Flying Solo USA in 2021. I had spent almost thirty years of my life living in regional South Australia, as my family moved to Mount Gambier when I was six years old—an upbringing spanning from primary school to mid- sixteen years in the farming regions of Kongorong. I had owned my house in Mount Gambier for ten years before moving to the big smoke. My property was registered in the name of my company. SAPOL, in criminal negligence to cover up and quit operations surrounding my life, allowed malicious accusations with no basis or facts to be spread to VICPOL and the AFP during the homicide investigation to seed, leading to the illegal acquisition of my sanctuary. My house, business location, pets' home, and ten years of my life were illegally acquisitioned for a cover-up. At the same time, SAPOL accused me of being a prostitute to paedophile police officers. Actions that led to myself being raped and assaulted numerous times before I resided in Adelaide. All the offences committed against me, the police allowed. Meanwhile, I watched Ice/methamphetamine dealers, domestic violence offenders, and sex offenders protected and called 'human resources' – informants—the police's personal gang of criminals and crimes they protect. The intentionally malicious and defamatory claims that I was a prostitute ruined my life severely from the year 2016 onwards, until I could no longer be ignored, as with all the truths I told in a relentless release of autobiographical content in self-defence of government-driven defamation, cover-ups, and terrorism being committed against my life and livelihood—public Information Disclosures. Malicious, disruptive actions and endless attempts of entrapment; I felt like I was living a cycle of extraordinary emergencies, always pushing me into near homelessness – police and government determined to turn an innocent, defenseless girl into their imaginary prostitute. My family had left me for dead. Without a stable residence in these circumstances, I fought alone for my survival and was lucky to find hotels at times until securing a safe rental where I could reside alone. Even when police torts led to my false incarceration, my parents provided no basic needs, support, or mental health support—all these choices were made to cover up sex offences.

So many things led to the reckless endangerment, mainly a Labor government-influenced cover-up of my whistleblowing. Other factors were my dad taking 10 odd grand ($10,000.00 AUD) from Phil, the President of the Gypsy Jokers (Adelaide/Mount Gambier), after the severe assault against him that I told Channel Seven News about, with family encouragement. SAPOL mishandled the serious assault via maladministration – paperwork and my dad taking the money complicated life A lot for me. The offenders submitted Guilty Pleas in court, the paperwork resulting in no jail time, as Dad informed me after court. No jail time, even though my dad suffered many broken bones, much dental damage, and could have died. My cousin was a police officer with SAPOL at the time, serving under the longstanding South Australian Police Commissioner, Malcom Hyde, who oversaw SAPOL from 1997 to 2012. A police commissioner who used my life and then abandoned the operation, seemingly upon retirement, when it became too difficult to protect himself from the consequences of his abuse of power and processes. An example I'm sure top officers set before him. One of these abuses was to appoint me as a police officer in numerous government department databases – blatant malfeasance endangering my life. Actions of a corrupt police force left me used against a gang of sexual offenders to be abused and sexually violated over and over again. The rumours of prostitution allowed and aided by police left me living in the aftermath of police criminal negligence and at the whim of crime. Crime that would not cease without a resolution to the malicious accusations with no basis or facts of sex industry work. My autobiography UGLY HEROS The Price Of Unlawful Enforcement (International publication) goes very in-depth into the decades of police operation fails, the abhorrent reckless endangerment, criminal negligence, neglect of duty of care, maladministration, malpractice, intentional and malicious torture, criminal conduct and irrefutable illegal actions of SAPOL and the Australian police force plus government department cover ups surrounding my life (historically) with the conclusion of the Autobiography written in real time. If you're interested in more details about the true crime novels documenting a solid decade of my life, read UGLY HEROS. Or Political Prisoner #192703, and don't write to me telling me 'heroes' is spelled with an 'e'. I know, and I don't care. If kids these days can write babe as bae, I can spell shit however the fuck I like if you still get the gist. Get around it.

Though this first book was always going to contain a bit of the sum of the three publications focused explicitly on True Crime ongoings, the purpose of the Anything but Ordinary series of autobiographies is to focus on the grouse stuff that makes me never want to commit suicide after being made a massive victim against my will. Always be a survivor and never a victim. Life is at least three hundred beautiful days a year - if you're unlucky, it is a few days or a few weeks less lovely, always focus on the beauty of life.

Although I was in a difficult position moving to Adelaide, living in the city was opening so many doors to get further involved in my extracurricular interests – Politics, Protest, and to study Law. As a very active volunteer in South Australia with a well-known, outspoken voice, I attended three protests within a few months of residing in Adelaide in 2021, regarding causes I support. Immediately captured on the front page of 'The Advertiser' Newspaper at the March4Justice Women's Rights Rally, and then following this protest, was chosen by indigenous leaders to stand beside speakers at the Raise The Age – Black Lives Matter protest, which was featured on 'NITV' with First Nations leadership.

Influence - Activism is right down my alley, and being in the city indeed presented plenty of opportunities to be influential just with my presence. To randomly quote Adam Brown of SAPOL regarding my whistleblowing, "You're influencing people" – Good! I hope so.

Additionally, at this stage, it was an honour to draw attention to my presence, as the 'Raise the Age' fight is so important to me—an exciting, purposeful, and peaceful protest aimed at creating a better world. I had the opportunity to support the Ambulance and Fire Service staff in their bid for adequate funding—a poignant protest that, under a responsible government, would have brought about change.

I was able to volunteer with political parties of interest in the big smoke – until malicious activity became evident in communications about me within political circles (e.g., New Liberals, Animal Justice Party), prompting me to withdraw from memberships when defamation began to circulate—motivation to start my own party. The Australian Freedom Party.

Events and protests are often held at Victoria Square in the heart of the city. Despite being of a petite build, in a crowd, I am pretty comfortable. One hundred and fifty-three centimetres tall and generally around fifty kilograms in weight, I am used to festival mosh pits and crowded pub/convention scenes.

Article 19 of the Declaration of Human Rights states, 'everyone has the right to freedom of opinion and expression; this right includes freedom to hold opinions without interference and to seek, receive and impart information and ideas through any media and regardless of frontiers.' The right to protest is a fundamental aspect of a democratic society. I was thrilled to be able to get involved with it all. Something that surprised me was the turnout of protesters. I was delighted to see so many people taking the time to exercise their rights and support one another in protest. March4Justice made its largest turnout yet that year. I was a little surprised by the different levels of society, including demographics and the interactions in the crowds, as many people gathered for a like-minded cause. Showing that bigotry can be dead if we want it to be. Different from the country town protest, where everyone knows everyone's collective voice and goes with it, the unity of all in the city seemed more organic

– very humbling. Protests display and create a genuine level of humanity and connection. It is where we remember that we are all the same, despite our colour, race, or religion. It truly dazzles me to see people set aside their differences for good. Our uniqueness, as beautiful as our similarities, is so underappreciated in day-to-day life. Mocking people out of conversation, gossip, and spite is nearly always unnecessary. I think the most damaging element of social media is the unaccountable keyboard warrior, thinking their venom is a public service. Hate breeds hate; we must be mindful of what we say, not just what we do. Apologise for wrongdoings, and even in retaliation, do not stoop to the lowest of levels. Emotional flex is best. Human nature is to have an emotional reaction. We need to channel our energy into positivity and understanding in our engagements; I believe this is the ultimate purpose of humanity. To embrace love. Loving one another and fostering a peaceful existence for a sustainable world.

When I moved to Adelaide, I had no car; my Mercedes-Benz in Mount Gambier was drivable but damaged beyond repair. Public transport was something I had rarely indulged in. Years before the move, I didn't know how to get off a tram, so I had to ring my brother, who had lived in the city, to ask him how to make it stop where I wanted to get off. Gaining my licence as soon as legally possible in South Australia, aged sixteen, it was a new experience to take the bus around the city in my thirties. I was still so nervous about travelling alone on public transport. It wasn't until after a couple of trips that the bus driver informed me that I was actually supposed to have a bus card to travel. Innocent little me, so clueless, he kindly instructed me where to go, what I needed, and I sat on the bus for approximately four and a half kilometres to the city from my residence for Free for the last time without my bus card.

I had walked the short distance to the city a few times without taking the bus. In the end, I found public transport rather pleasant and convenient for most trips. The convenience and environmental contributions of the bus trip led me to use the service for six months, and even after purchasing a new car. Jumping on the bus was easy; I could attend to emails on my phone, the bus stop was conveniently close, and it was good for the environment. All wins and so normal to city folk! The place was an amusement park to live in, like the live events I used to attend on weekends. Adelaide is a lovely place to live. Ranked the ninth most livable city in the world in the Economist Intelligence Unit's 2025 Global Livability Index.

I purchased a little city vehicle, a Kia Rio. My living expenses and plans influenced the purchase of an economical vehicle. A cute car with a few extra accessories, including roof racks, it looked sporty and was a perfect choice, which should have been an easy sale when the time came to fly out to the United States.

As the vehicle was a business purchase, I immediately added a bit of Barbwire Noose bling.

Adding some stickers and signage, nothing excessive, as the car was initially bought as a short- term asset. The vehicle was a lifesaving purchase in the end, enabling me to flee the numerous malicious actions I faced due to the police force's intentional criminal negligence to obstruct justice in desperate cover-up operations—life-threatening malfeasance and conspired efforts to discredit a whistleblower.

Saving money in the city was more difficult than in the country, but I managed. My living expenses were much higher than living in Mount Gambier, and now with a plan to travel and possibly move to America, New York City, as soon as possible in 2021, I got a credit card and was on my way to the USA until I wasn't.

The highlights of city living are that every weekend, there were Sports, Music, and cultural events when I lived in the state's capital city. I did a little sports writing online and enjoyed watching the footy and cricket matches as well. Aware of the large Indian community in Adelaide, this being my heritage, it was wonderful to be able to attend these events.

2016 Clipsal 500 Adelaide TVC

I found growing up in a regional town that racism was silent but prominent. In the city, I was able to embrace my Indian heritage without the snickers and sneering of small minds, which were rarely said to one's face.

My appearance is Australian – mainly Caucasian, my olive skin gives away an ethnic descent, often not picked as Indian initially. Asked "Are you Italian?" more often than not, I am related to many Italians through marriage on my mother's side of the family, but I'm not Italian. My Dad is of British origin, while my mum has British Indian roots, including my grandfather, who is also of German descent. Absolutely loving Indian culture, I enjoyed attending the Harvest and Indian Mela Festivals of 2021.

By October 2021, I was forced to leave Adelaide after a rapist threatened me. Trying to bribe me to remove the report I made against him by sending out-of- context text to my then-fiancée's Facebook. After being assaulted and raped while residing in Adelaide, I no longer felt safe in a state where a judge had acknowledged police were committing institutional abuse and clear torts against me. Yet, no

Royal Commission into SAPOL was called. These incidents were all reported to the Norwood Police Station near where I resided most of the time while living in Adelaide (2021). All reports met with police criminal negligence and notions that they were allowing these crimes to be committed. Police disrupted my plans to fly out to the USA for NYFW2021, encouraged sexual violence, and had a repetitive plot of homelessness. The travel restrictions of the coronavirus faced by the globe solidified my choice to stay in Australia at this time. As a survivor, not a life victim, life goes on unless you're dead.

After November 2021 had passed, I planned to return to Adelaide despite still living in reckless endangerment conditions, as it was the best option for my clothing brand. Fabric stores were basically non-existent where I relocated in the Northern Territory, in the city of Alice Springs. The country city was of a size like Mount Gambier, without the broad shopping range and sewing supplies.

I could only purchase satins and basic haberdashery locally; there was nothing suitable for extravagant couture collections, nor for pursuing New York Fashion Week (NYFW) prospects. The roads were flooded, so my desire to return to the big smoke was severely delayed. Barbwire Noose's turnover was severely affected by the circumstances of whistleblowing. I ended up taking on a position as a bar attendant, working as a bartender at the bars of the famous Casino featured in the iconic film Priscilla, Queen of the Desert. The role was busy, demanding, but also rather fun, so I shelved the idea of heading back to Adelaide after my employment probation period and planned to attend NYFW 2022 without a collection.

Instead, I would wear a design I had created for NYFW 2021 and plan to wear other couture creations throughout the event. The casino hours and wages allowed me to easily save for a trip to NYFW 2022 while continuing to invest, seek investors, and expand Barbwire Noose®.

City living now back to country again, I focused on what I could achieve and released a collection of streetwear (2022) called 'Protest Graff', which further represented my activism, along with the brand's representation of Freedom and Human Rights. This collection was also produced without the use of vinyl and machinery I did not have on hand.

While seeking refuge in the Northern Territory, technically again, I took my brand to the country runway and participated in the 2022 Sustainable Couture Runway event. Barbwire Noose showcases an upcycled collection of my NYFW2021 design pieces. The garments showcased on the country runway had been featured for sale for a month of 2021 in New York as part of Barbwire Noose NYFW 2021 selection. An event that Alice Springs has had the bragging rights to for over a decade and a half. The event engages many talented locals and visitors who produce sustainable fashion and showcases sustainable designs. My collection was a last-minute entry, which did not matter aside from the fact that we had to find our own models (volunteers). I was lucky enough that a couple of my gorgeous colleagues from the Casino modelled my BN Couture threads, as well as myself. The event was enjoyable, and all the models did an outstanding job. The energy of my work colleagues, coupled with their enthusiasm, made it such a pleasure to have my designs showcased by them – so spectacularly. To participate in the Sustainable Couture event at the end of June, I adjusted my preparation schedule and left for NYFW 2022 relatively close to the event. I made a quick visit to Adelaide to take an intervention order out against a stalking SAPOL police officer, Constantinos David Kyriacou (SAPOL ID 40657), whose obsession with me seemed to cause as much trouble as it did good. Irrefutably, in 2024, when an incarceration tort with his name on it nearly pushed me to the refuge of suicide. While passing through Adelaide, I put some belongings I was not taking to New York (USA) into storage with National Storage, who later attempted to steal numerous belongings and disposed of Barbwire Noose® manufacturing equipment.

As September approached, NYWF2022 Fall/Winter, I had saved enough money to attend NYFW and indulge in the New York culture, plus the broader USA, for at least a couple of months. Planning to visit and physically see my fiancée on this trip, also. I purchased flights for August 13th, and some initial accommodation in New York, not knowing that VICPOL was continuing to engage in tortious conduct. Issuing a ridiculous number of warrants and investigating me over the years, malicious and intentional torts based on illegal and defamatory statements, and intervention orders created in maladministration, really only to suppress the truth. Everyone knows police are creeps anyway, you'd think they'd change by this day and age, and would not spend millions on cover-ups. This is one of the many examples of why cops get called pigs. Their attitude that they are privileged and can commit criminality. Instead of making it to NYFW2022, I found myself illegally detained for almost a month and placed in Dame Phyllis Frost Centre (DPFC) (refer to this chapter for the details). I, having engaged legal representation regarding the behaviour of both VICPOL and SAPOL with a civil torts claim in July 2022, make the facts that VICPOL engaged numerous police forces to traumatise me an ever more surreal and unpredictable reality until I lived it. All these investigations, disruptions, and criminal negligence were just torts to protect sex crimes. Furthermore, I was a victim of paedophilia in governance, and I was the one subjected to the injustice. A tort is a civil wrong that causes a claimant to suffer loss or harm, resulting in legal liability for the person who commits the tortious act. VICPOL engaged in actions of assault, battery, false imprisonment, breach of the Privacy Act, intimidation against my person, and even theft of property. In 2024, SAPOL engaged in long, more life- threatening incarceration torts. The book Political Prisoner #192703, dedicated to this time, documents an unflinching firsthand account of injustice, resilience, and the pursuit of truth. Through raw reflections, real-time quotes, and bold insight, I authored not just a memoir but a message calling for systemic change, uplifting the human spirit, and urging us to confront the realities inside Australia's detention system.

The trusting from city to country living was exhausting, let alone country to country, and after VICPOL committed an un-compensable level of torts, to which I'm sure sex offending officer Damian Ferrari and his merry mutts are proud of, I returned to Adelaide very briefly. In mid-September 2022, I had to return to South Australia via Alice Springs as I needed to collect my business car, which I had in long-term airport parking, ready for my return after attending NYFW2022.

The fact that I was allowed to travel to the USA, not knowing I was going to be made to return to be put through the courts by VICPOL, is an outrageous tort. Then, to find I was being put through court because of malfeasance to cover up their malpractice and maladministration to protect sex offending and domestic violence offending committed by VICPOL officer Damian H.Ferrari (DOB1966), outraged me. All this harassment, amounting to false incarceration, was an abomination. A report I made in November 2018 to a female detective, clearly not good at her job or of high integrity, led to incarceration. The tort carried out was so vile that I was incarcerated in the conditions of US prisons. Incarceration was so traumatic to me that simply adding the harassment to my torts civil claim against them wasn't justice enough. I instructed my lawyers to take the case to trial if an adequate and swift resolution could not be attained. I also wanted a written apology from all VICPOL police officers involved, as I was demanding from SAPOL. Acknowledge the wrongdoings and really change the culture of policing so this never happens again. My passport was flagged by law enforcement in Hawaii, USA, where police engaged in perverting the course of justice internationally with their severe defamation. My move to the city and back to country living was more than underwhelming during reckless endangerment over numerous states. From August 17th, after entering the state of Victoria, I was forced to reside in Melbourne for basically a month against my will. Missing the simplicity of regional living became just missing living a real, free life. Enduring nearly a decade of reckless endangerment (at least) was bad enough without being jerked across the country by corrupt police activity, creating further defamation, trauma upon myself, and irrefutable civil tort claims.

After seeing the dirty walls of DPFC, I was placed into a room as emergency housing in Melbourne, which was actually a more pleasant experience than not (except for the bed bugs!). It was a hotel located next to Monash University, and it actually provided free meals (although not five-star quality, with some of it clearly donated) for its guests, which I thought was kind and had never seen before. I only had to walk approximately 10 minutes to the grocery store, which, for the most part, is what I did. The staff were very friendly and respectful, plus the room had a bath, which I was surprised and pleased to see. I bathed numerous times, soaking away the weeks at DPFC in a hot bath with some oils and a few beverages. A bathtub, seriously, was a blessing during such a torturous and traumatic ordeal. The experience showed me that I had picked the proper capital city for myself and my brand. Not that I have ever actually resided in Melbourne, the vibe, the music scene, the graffiti, all screaming Barbwire Noose®. The state of Victoria is a dictatorship compared to most other states, riddled with shit roads and serious crime acts.

Living in Adelaide gave Barbwire Noose so many opportunities. I had run billboards in Times Square, New York, in 2020. From Adelaide for NYFW 2021, I advertised in the USA, where my ex-fiancée was located. I was able to progress a little again briefly in 2021 despite SAPOL's announced quote "cover-up" of their use of sex work, including sex offences against minors. How heroically lame.

I reopened a business letterbox in the capital city as per Barbwire Noose's incorporation direction. Not on Sturt Street CBD – the first City letterbox, acquired years before - and this post office was now closed. Advertising was easier, deliveries came fast, and I had an abundance of inspiration to design around me. I was set up to settle in where I was if I was not successful in New York. Pretty sure I would be successful; Australia will always be home.

The judge acknowledged the incarceration tort on the 5th of September 2022. I was also encouraged to continue forward with my writing and pursuit of a legal degree. Missing NYFW2022 is entirely VICPOL, and the police forces involved are at fault. That said, my very brief forced stay in Melbourne led me to conclude that I'd rather live in Adelaide, in my home state of South Australia.

I missed the trees, the slow, simple, casual living of Mount Gambier almost immediately—the ease of traffic and parking. Yet, I can confidently say I felt at home amongst the noise and bustle.

Chapter Three

'A Life of Endless Lives'

One Testing Experience Too Many. A Life of Endless Lives and A Yellow Curtain Blind.

Here is a kind of randomly listed recollection of times I recall nearly dying or have been in unpredictable circumstances that have been life-threatening.

I was 8 years old when Dad got me and my brother our first motorbike, a Honda with three gears. I jumped on first. Thank God for helmets, as using the brakes didn't occur, and I went headfirst over the handlebars, smashing my head on a Mount Gambier stone brick slab.

Growing up on a farm is not just dangerous when riding a motorbike; I was nearly bitten by a snake twice while growing up on the farm. I jumped off the concrete front porch one day in front of my dad and neighbour, exactly where I leaped was a yellow- bellied brown snake, its head reared, ready to strike.

Another farm moment was when I was saved by the family dog, 'Nails'. I was going for a walk in the peace and serenity of the country landscape, which was my backyard, the paddock surrounded by pine tree forests. I screamed and stood still as soon as I saw the snake. Dad taught us growing up to make no sudden movements around snakes and to slowly back away. 'Nails' was named Nails by Dad when he was a puppy, as he got run over by the car and was okay – 'Tough as Nails'. Nails pounced on the brown snake, allowing me to move away and continued to attack the snake due to my frightened reaction. Dad ran out as soon as he heard my scream, within minutes, to kill the snake. The snake slithered off through the paddock's grasses. With the scrub nearby, we did not continue to look for it. The dog was bitten, but survived the incident.

Another life-threatening moment was a targeted attack in 2004 by some feral bitches. One of my brother's exes came to my house looking for my brother. I nearly had my head cracked open on a concrete-filled pylon; the only thing that stopped them was me finally skitzing out to retaliate and defend myself. The biggest of the ferals yelled out as I walked back to the property I rented, "I'll get my Gypsy Joker Uncle to rape you". A disgusting, paedophile protecting group of pigs describes a lot of that bunch of so-called bikers. Bikers are frowned upon for protecting paedophilia globally, apparently. This type of behavior makes you wonder what they really stand for.

I've been lucky in numerous car accidents; there are a few standouts that nearly saw the end of me. The first was on a highway, where my car spun out of control and stopped hanging over a fence, a metre above the ground. The fence was poling railings with sports cage wiring. The pole from the fence was headed straight for my head. I was watching it as it came for the windscreen. Miraculously, it bentupwards and over the bonnet instead of piercing the front windscreen and drilling through my forehead.

Another car accident was a car that was rear-ended and pushed through my lounge room window. I was eating a Subway chicken salad bowl with avocado when I heard a crashing bang behind me. I moved away from the noise, leaving my Subway with my favourite parts of the salad bowl - the chicken and the avocado portion left where I sat. I had been saving the meat and added extra avocado for last, I watched the best of my meal get crushed by the frame of my lounge room window. The wooden framing and window were dislodged from the wall as the car propelled into the lounge room. My Subway being where I sat, I was lucky I moved; otherwise, I would have been split in half from the skull by the wooden window frame. I was milliseconds and centimetres away from being divided in half by the debris of the vehicle colliding with my house. Personally, I would have aimed for the car in front of my house, not the neighbour's lounge – yes, the driver of the vehicle which ended up in my lounge room was also my neighbour—joking as they exited the car, that they would use the door next time. I was distraught and cried until my parents arrived approximately thirty-odd minutes later. The bong and weed bowl survived.

An ex, with an out-of-control addiction to the laced hydro cannabis that circulated Mount Gambier, South Australia, for years – the buds laced with methamphetamines and insecticides. This ex- boyfriend, a generation of friends, and boys with domestic violence tendencies years later, were revealed after he nearly killed me in a car crash. In his domestic violence, his narcissistic behaviour turned violent as I refused to purchase him hydro weed. He deliberately crashed his car, accelerating out of control into the side of the road, travelling at a speed of at least eighty (80) kilometres per hour in a suburban area zoned at sixty (60) kilometers per hour. He hurled his Ford Falcon, with me on the passenger side, at a stobie pole. The back tyre burst, changing the course of the vehicle, and saving my life.

In 2012, I was strangled during a domestic violence incident, with my life threatened by the piece of shit as I bashed at his hands to release them. He confessed his crime to an on-duty SAPOL officer directly after committing the offence. The interaction between the two men caught on camera at a service station on the same road I lived on. CCTV even apparently captures the offence, yet for over a decade the offence remains uncharged by SAPOL, as with the sex crime I reported committed against me as a minor. Life-threatening acts, two offenders affray linked, and no charges, is SAPOL pushing for me to take my life via suicide like the victims of powerful men globally? God knows, and so do they.

A domestic violence incident 2013 occurred in Adelaide. I saw myself again in the passenger side of a car being driven by a then partner, being used as a weapon like the Ford Falcon. This vehicle was a Ute heading towards a tree. The police were called, yet the domestic violence offender went uncharged; instead, the offender was placed in a mental health hospital, getting away with nearly killing me in a car crash because he was a SAPOL informant.

Domestic violence in Australia is ending the lives of innocent women and destroying so many families. I basically stopped having relationships in 2014 and seriously could have joined a convent.

Living through severe reckless endangerment due to malicious criminal negligence by police, due to torts after being used and utilised by police, is dangerous business. Especially when nearly every facet engaged by police was malfeasance surrounding your life, everything is a lie, and everything is a cover-up. From telling felons I was an informant, to their pursuit to make me homeless, the documentation is irrefutable that Australian police officers of all forces intentionally compromised my life in hopes that I would commit suicide or be murdered.

From SAPOL Police Commissioner Malcom Hyde, regarding the utilisation of my life in relation to Hans and Luke Hubert Scheidl of Mount Gambier/Renmark, South Australia. Followed by SAPOL Paul Griffiths sharing evidence without disciplinary action, which compromised the investigation into a homicide, to malicious accusations of no basis or facts regarding sex work, several attempts at entrapment, perverting the course of justice, and coercion of suicide via institutional abuses and attempts/forced homelessness, to the blatantly intentional neglect of my safety by police officers in general. It's been a hectic ride, not allowing the cover-up of sex offending in Australian government departments to kill me.

Without bragging *cough*, I can drive; thus far, in life, one of the highest speeds I've travelled is approximately 212km - the circumstances were hectic. I was being harassed and intimidated by police activities who, at this time, without due authority, were conducting surveillance on me. I must say, it was nighttime, and seriously, do not do stupid shit like this. The police were engaging in some very corrupt, illegal activity, as expressed. Their criminal negligence, which was recklessly endangering my life, was out of control – I thought I was going to die from their outrageous operations in an extraordinary emergency. The speed felt like a necessity at this time- self-defense, surrounded by setups and cover- ups spilling over from a homicide case overseen by the Australian Federal Police (AFP) force.

Custody in Melbourne, when I was illegally detained for nothing really, a few texts telling a corrupt cop to get fucked after I reported him for rape and domestic violence, I nearly saw my heart stop. G4S St Kilda Road, the location where I almost lost my life, my Human Rights, and the justice system was severely compromised. Over 24 hours (recorded on camera), I was fed at least 16 painkillers, a mix of Panadol and Nurofen tablets, four (4) at a time. Two (2) Panadol and two (2) Nurofen per dose, topped with oxycodone and Valium – I had never consumed oxycodone or Valium in my life. At the time, I was no more than 51kg in weight, and my heart nearly stopped on the night of the 19th of August 2022.

I had been assaulted in the Northern Territory by a gangster wannabe with a history of assaulting smaller women, detailed in UGLY HEROS, after all, this book is supposed to be mostly light-hearted. And lots of it is.

Personally, I was so drunk after eating nothing all day and hanging out in the heat. I don't recall much of the incident; that said, I was assaulted due to malicious accusations with no basis or facts spread by police, wannabe gangsters, and petty gossip within communities. After the assault, I chose not to be floating about Alice Springs making friends, as I had no idea what their agenda was going to be.

I met Darren Nixon, also known as Bryan Porker - Life of Bryan, via my social media, while I was recklessly endangered at the end of 2022. With cannabis charges his only claim to fame, an NTPOL arrest years before our lives crossed paths. He seemed harmless enough and was a charismatic person. He had an ambition to apply for Big Brother and had spent most of his life travelling around Australia. Hanging out with Bryan, I could have been left in the desert with no food, water, or vehicle, on native land with no mobile range.

A bit of Bryan's story, told with his permission, is that he was adopted into a loving family from McBride's Hospital. Having at this stage never met his biological parents, he expressed how fortunate he was in his adoption, an upbringing he recalls fondly. Known as Bryan in life, born Darren Nixon, he has travelled Australia for over 30 years. I travelled with Bryan on many road trips during my Human rights fight for justice against government departments' cover-up of sex crimes. Having led a worldly life, like me, he seemed happy-go-lucky and would talk to all walks of life. I found Bryan to be humble, a silent leader, wise, and generally caring. Meeting Bryan during the legalization of marijuana, we shared many laughs over a joint. Further details on the marijuana charge, Bryan suffered the injustice of incarceration regarding the legalization of the drug marijuana for a quantity of 'less than a kilo'. He was charged with possession of a commercial quantity by NTPOL. Prohibition laws regarding marijuana are evidently unjustified, with many countries legalising and expunging this draconian-led governance, pursuing charges against innocent citizens. Self-medication isn't against constitutional principles (The six foundation principles are democracy, the rule of law, the separation of powers, federalism, nationhood, and rights balanced by responsibilities) and is UnAustralian.

Bryan's actions in the end were unacceptable; he let drugs and fear rule his decisions, and he crossed the line, sexually assaulting me on the ass and attempting to access under my clothes— unforgivable disrespect and offending against me. I reported to SAPOL, and they refused to take a statement from me. By 2025, Bryan was in prison in

Alice Springs for possessing a large quantity of drugs, I was told.

Reckless endangerment due to malicious accusations with no factual basis had become a constant danger, no matter where I lived. Men for years had planned, plotted, and stalked me to commit sexual violence since SAPOL used me as rape bait. The police, overall, had intentionally allowed and engaged in criminal negligence in investigations and operations surrounding me, with there even being efforts of entrapment in charges executed by police informants. Conduct so calculated that you knew police had set people up to cover up their crimes and failed operations before. Like criminals endangering my life, then deny, deny, deny. It was seriously Surreal living through the extensive efforts of malfeasance police, irrefutably engaged to cover up their uses and abuses of my life, plus sexual crime in governance. I could have died in the Northern Territory with the highly damaging defamation circulating. At the time, I pushed to reside in a state with the highest crime rates in Australia—Alice Springs had the highest city crime rate. The place where you go if you're wanted or unwanted, they say. Stuck also by floods, not just reckless endangerment, 2021/2022, I had been bar attending at the casino where the police's damaging defamation circulated irrefutably. I had been employed only a few months after rejecting this loser AFP member who lived next door in his fuck buddy proposal. Trying to impress me by saying he's been in the Rebels clubhouse, I found 'lad' to be suffering from little man's syndrome from where I stood. The police forces, including the Australian Federal Police (AFP) in Australia, after the global 'me too' movement and extensive policing of Jeffrey Epstein, spent decades and millions of misappropriated tax dollars trying to cover up their use of prostitutes, including children. No AFP police member was going to really impress me at this stage of the justice crusade. They were half the problem, and I knew it; I just had to prove it. In 2022, I did, when the AFP took the opportunity to assist VICPOL to conduct a tort against me. State authorities require AFP approval to conduct investigations across borders, as well as for extradition. It is irrefutable that these three states, South Australia (SAPOL), Victoria (VICPOL), and Northern Territory (NTPOL), in conjunction with the AFP, were making life-threatening efforts to pervert the course of justice and cover up sex crimes committed and allowed under numerous government departments. Instead of flying out to New York, I made it to Hawaii, where I was incarcerated by the tort, which eventually sent me back to seek refuge in Alice Springs. Thanks, New York 'Hilton' Hotel, for the refund, I'll make it one day!! At this time, NTPOL was running intentionally negligent investigations leading to police criminal negligence and further reckless endangerment to my life. On what basis, none. I've asked numerous times for my FOI, and at the start of 2022, I was told by an NTPOL police officer that there was no FOI on me aside from the assault I reported. Before travelling with Life of Bryan on a sponsorship trip with my brand in 2023, we received texts with threats about incarceration made to persons by NTPOL, texts saying I was an informant, etc. These malicious accusations stemming from orchestrated police investigations and circulated by shit humans were a replica of my experience in South Australia. Police were desperate in 2023 under Commissioner AFP Reece Kershaw, Grant Stevens SAPOL, Shane Patton VICPOL, and Jamie Chalker NTPOL, who still tried to cover up sex crimes despite all the evidence presented outing the cover-up conspiracy between states and federal representatives over the years. Threatening and disruptive investigation tactics, my fellow traveller actually knew well, an influence that seemed to have Bryan start travelling with less endangerment to my life. Only just. We were on the road touring when my property manager, whom I awkwardly witnessed part of a Domestic violence dispute between him and his partner, abruptly ended my lease. The landlord, who has a history of infidelity with his KFC staff, was in support of the dodgy decision. Making up a threat of arson, when these men's rhetoric endangered my life. Some people are legally sane yet fucking insane.

Remember the Alice Springs KFC owner who campaigned for his store to be awarded the coveted Michelin Star? That guy tried to say something about erratic behaviour to me!? WTF. A nut that cheats on his gorgeous wife in a small town and asks for a Michelin Star for KFC – ambition is good, this is a little 'are you snorting too much cocaine, Sammy boy'. Unsurprisingly, Michelin said no. I made it

68

clear that I would not tolerate the abrupt cancellation of the lease without a fight. Especially as he was allowing a domestic violence felon on parole at the time to keep a lease over me, the felon, knowing the dirty facts of both men, and also responsible for the threatening texts about arson, not me. I could not help but wonder if I was being pushed into almost homelessness again because of these men's indecency and sexual indecency, not just police desperate to pervert the course of justice. I had made legal enquiries earlier in the year about breaches of the Tenancy Act regarding the living environment and privacy. Flying out to the USA and my focus on the Sustainable Couture Runway, plus work at the casino, made the audio recordings where I lived a last priority on my to-do list. At the time of this abrupt lease cancellation, VICPOL was apparently again trying to investigate me. Oppression and endless malicious maladministration to try and stop me publishing the truth to cover up the irrefutable sex crimes their police commit, and my reports against one, like SAPOL. I thought it odd that VICPOL would get AFP approval to investigate over the border after committing the severest of torts. It seems they may not have. If they did not, someone had indeed called a favour via state police and encouraged whatever shit informants and humans they could find to partake in the defamation campaign. Deja vu to me, I felt like an expert at seeing entrapment coming from a mile away. VICPOL in 2023 was facing a five- million-dollar legal tort claim after years of malfeasance, breaches of privacy, stalking, neglectful investigations, criminal negligence, attempts at entrapment, and false incarceration. Scary shit most say. I wasn't scared or allowed to really be, Fear Is the Root of All Weakness®. Yet, some people thought I should be, as they had watched the police for years cause much turmoil. Though it did seem VICPOL was more desperate to try to bring life to the defamation of prostitution, more hopeless than SAPOL. While the police force's malicious, intentional criminal negligence and deliberate neglectful investigations compromised my safety, travelling was a fun distraction from the seriousness of whistleblowing.

Like a cat with nine lives, so far, I have survived it all. I live every day happy to be living and happy to die. Evidently, God loves me; I literally say that, and it has been evident as I've served humanity with my life thus far.

Chapter Four

'Teaching'

Everything is wondrous as a child. I feel very blessed that I have been able to spend nearly two decades around children. Kids do say the darndest things. Their thirst for life experiences and inquisitive nature nurture the soul back into a time when everything was exciting. Even the fear of learning things like riding a bike for the first time or learning to swim was that extra bit more exciting as a child, as opposed to being an adult. Swimming is a lifesaving skill, and I am so proud to have equipped so many children with this skill.

Aquatics Teaching as a teenager forced me to grow up quickly; if you wanted to keep your job in a small town, you needed to act responsibly. The older sister in my family, I was used to responsibility. Often taking the mature role around the house, I was already very sensible. Teaching enhances that sense of responsibility and grooms you into a person (if you wish or care) with respectable public conduct, considering the watchful judgment of others.

Especially when it's judgment from parents staring down at you through the glass of the observation room as you teach their child, who is still a teenager at home with you. Many students say hi in the local supermarket. I've never been caught with my finger up my nose. Thank God my parents taught me good manners.

I think it's the best job in the world, rewarding and fun. I can think of nothing better than educating people, especially kids, on water safety and the skill of swimming and playing in a pool. Aquatics Teaching has been my primary job and my secondary job for countless years of my life, and is the job I know best. I want to think it's where my best skill sets lie, unfortunately, this is not true.

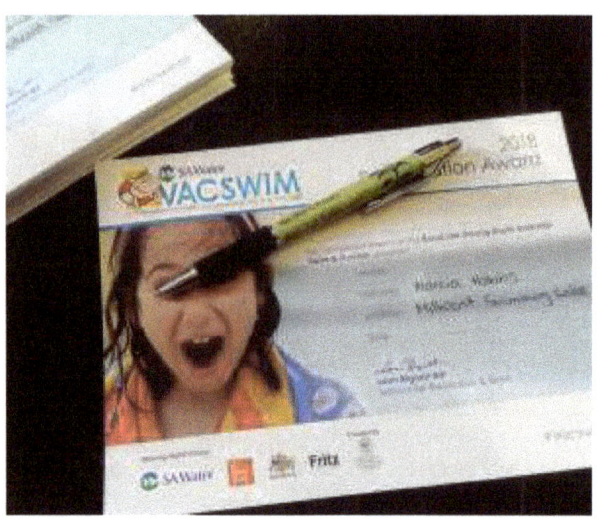

I'm an academic, and my most excellent skills fall within the realm of litigation, specifically the law and being a voice of reason, as well as protest.

The AUSTSWIM qualification is nationally recognised, and

I have basically every qualification you can obtain under its credentials. Swimming and Water Safety, Infant and Preschool Aquatics, Towards Competitive Strokes, Aquatics for People with a Disability - I can teach it all. Very proud of how good I am at the occupation. My years teaching swimming have been one of the great highlights of my life.

Taught by one of Australia's leading coaches and an outstanding woman in the profession of Swim Coaching, my training to become a Swim Teacher was undoubtedly more complex than most. Everyone who worked at 'The Waterhole' indoor heated pool of Mount Gambier was trained to perfection to work as a Swim Teacher at the facility.

I was a student at 'The Waterhole' during high school, then after an invitation from management, I started voluntary work. After a period of time, when I turned sixteen, I was classed as a proficient aquatic educator. I taught myself how to tumble-turn and numerous other skills that I did not aspire to as a student, but could teach once I qualified in aquatics. The occupation, such fun, I would apply to work at pools wherever I resided. Receiving much praise for my aquatics teaching, I am humbled and grateful that the impressions I left were positive and enduring, teaching a lifesaving life skill.

"Children are like wet cement. Whatever falls on them makes an impression." - Haim Ginott.

These days, I teach social activism, self-care, marketing, and courage – I hope. Here's a blog excerpt from my website, titled 'Empowering Change Through Human Rights Activism.'

I'm not here to sugarcoat it. Change is brutal. It's raw. It's relentless. And if you think activism is some polite conversation over tea, you're dead wrong. Activism is a battlefield. It's a war cry. It's the voice of the unheard screaming until the walls crumble. I've lived it, breathed it, and fought tooth and nail for it. This isn't just about waving signs or posting hashtags. This is about empowering change through real, gritty, unapologetic action.

If you want to make a dent in this world, you need to understand the activism strategies for social impact that actually work. No fluff. No distractions. Just pure, unfiltered power.

Why Activism Strategies for Social Impact Matter

Let me be blunt: passion alone won't cut it. You can scream your lungs out, but if you don't have a strategy, you're just noise. Activism without a plan is like a ship without a rudder - it drifts, it falters, it sinks.

So what does a strategy look like? It's a blueprint. A roadmap. A tactical approach that turns outrage into results. It's about knowing your audience, your message, and your battlefield. It's about leveraging every tool at your disposal - from grassroots organising to digital campaigns, from fashion statements to legal battles.

Take the example of Marcia BNoose, a powerhouse who uses her personal brand and fashion line, Barbwire Noose, to amplify voices that are often silenced. She's not just talking the talk; she's walking the walk, blending style with substance to challenge Australia's governance and disability sectors. That's strategy. That's impact.

- Identify your cause clearly: What injustice are you fighting? Be specific
- Build a community: Change is collective. Find your tribe.

- Use multiple platforms: Social media, art, fashion, literature - all are weapons.

- Engage with policymakers: Don't just protest outside their doors; demand

  a seat at the table.

- Measure your impact: Track progress, adapt, and push harder.

The Power of Personal Branding in Activism

You want to be heard? Then you need to be seen. Not just physically, but as a symbol. Personal branding in activism is not vanity; it's a weapon. It's how you carve out space in a crowded world.

Marcia BNoose's journey is a masterclass in this. She didn't just become a voice; she became *the* voice. Her fashion line, Barbwire Noose, isn't just clothing—it's a statement. It's rebellion stitched into fabric. It's a walking manifesto. When you wear that brand, you're not just dressing up; you're declaring war on injustice.

This is how you build momentum. You create a visual identity that resonates. You make your activism tangible. People don't just support causes; they rally behind symbols.

Here's how you can harness personal branding for your cause:

Define your core message - What do you stand for?

Create a visual identity - Logos, colours, styles that reflect your mission.

Be authentic - People smell fake from a mile away.

Use storytelling - Share your journey, struggles, and victories.

Collaborate with creatives - Fashion, art, music - all amplify your voice.

What is an example of a human rights activist?

When I say human rights activist, I'm not talking about some distant figure in history books. I'm referring to individuals who fight for justice every single day—people who refuse to stay silent when the world looks the other way.

Take Malala Yousafzai. Shot for demanding education for girls, yet she rose from the ashes, louder and fiercer than ever. Or consider Greta Thunberg, who turned climate despair into a global movement with nothing but her voice and a sign. These are not just activists; they are symbols of relentless courage.

Closer to home, Marcia BNoose embodies this spirit. She fights for the voiceless in Australia's governance and disability sectors, using every tool at her disposal - from her published works to her fashion line. She's proof that activism is not confined to protests; it's a lifestyle, a commitment, a revolution.

If you want to be an activist, ask yourself: *What am I willing to risk? How far will I go?*
Because activism demands everything.

How to Turn Passion into Action: Practical Steps

Feeling fired up? Good. But passion without action is just noise. Here's how you turn that fire into a raging inferno that can't be ignored.

- **Educate Yourself Relentlessly**: Know the laws, the history, the players. Knowledge is power.

- **Network Like Your Life Depends On It**: Connect with other activists, organisations, and allies.

- **Use Social Media Strategically**: It's not just about posting; it's about engaging, educating, and mobilising.

- **Organise Events and Campaigns**: From local meetups to global online campaigns, get people involved.

- **Hold Authorities Accountable**: Demand transparency, justice, and reform.

- **Self-Care is Not Optional**: Burnout kills movements. Take care of your mind and body.

Remember, activism is a marathon, not a sprint. You need stamina, resilience, and a great deal of grit.

Why Fashion and Activism Are a Perfect Match

You might think fashion and activism are worlds apart. But they're not. Fashion is a language. It's a way to communicate without words. It's a walking billboard for your beliefs.

Marcia BNoose's Barbwire Noose line is a perfect example. It's edgy, unapologetic, and loud. It challenges norms and forces conversations. When you wear activist fashion, you're not just making a style choice; you're making a statement. You're saying, "I stand for something bigger than myself."

Fashion can:

- **Raise awareness**: Bold designs catch eyes and spark questions.

- **Fund activism**: Proceeds can support causes.

- **Build community**: Wearing the same message creates solidarity.

- **Challenge stereotypes**: Break down barriers with style.

If you want to empower change, don't underestimate the power of what you wear.

The Road Ahead: Keep Fighting, Keep Rising

Here's the brutal truth: the fight for justice never ends. It's exhausting, infuriating, and often thankless. But it's also the most important battle you'll ever fight.

If you want to be part of this revolution, you need to commit. You need to be relentless. You need to use every tool, every strategy, every ounce of your being to push for change.

And if you ever doubt yourself, remember this: every movement started with one voice.

One person who refused to be silent. One person said, "Enough."

If you want to learn more about how to channel your energy into effective human rights activism, look no further than those who live it every day. Marcia BNoose is not just a name; she's a force. A leader. A beacon for those who dare to dream of a better world.

So, what are you waiting for? The time to act is now. The world needs your voice. Your passion. Your fight.

Chapter Five

'Lover to Lover'

"No one is born hating another person because of the colour of his skin, or his background, or his religion. People must learn to hate, and if they can learn to hate, they can be taught to love, for love comes more naturally to the human heart than its opposite." - Nelson Mandela, Long Walk to Freedom.

I moved out of my home with a boy I thought I might marry; we broke up, and I was immediately dating another whom I actually thought I'd marry. I was wrong about both and about the few relationships that followed, a few involving Domestic Violence relationships, and the release of a private intimate video – revenge porn, almost put me off men entirely.

Relationships had been secondary since 2014, which is why this chapter is lover to lover because a lot of it was something and nothing all at once: wrong place, wrong time, mainly me not being interested in complicating my life, red tape, not marriage material, and again that lack of interest in a partner I have.

Writing this book, I was engaged to my lover for life, my moon. With no intention to marry him. Love and support him, yes, fuck my life over – not so much the plan. Mrs Marcia Anita Enmon was so close to being my reality—two souls who were destined to connect in our lifetimes. Yet not destined to spend our lives together. He was the man I wanted. All I wanted. Finding the man who saved my sanity in 2014 was like being blind with shitty guides. A person who was present but not fully engaged the entire time. A meeting of souls in a travesty of destruction. Aligned and connected with a mind as Amazing and Immature as mine at times. Too old to use the excuses of pure stupidity, too young to be past mistakes and naivety. The non-stereotypical stereotype structure of our lives, as viewed through social media, leads us to judge each other, and for the most part, we like what we see. A distant friendship between Australia and America turned to love. A love made of the universe that had our growth intertwined by something so profound in the purpose of our existences - if you believe in that stuff (clearly, I do). We are deluded by the delusion that our existence as humans is subjective. Perhaps you're the only person I've ever truly loved; maybe I've loved everyone and never truly loved myself.

A Freemason touched my heart in 2015; he was also a man who showed me how greedy for power men really are. An unexpected love built through a trauma bond. It was such a confusing engagement of emotions. So, I'm in love with my ex- fiancée, but I'm not at all willing to acknowledge that to him. Telling him his version of Love was just Lust, which is precisely what I thought about the Freemason as he floated around my life. A man nine years older than me - something I had never considered as a prospect before. His brash approach was slightly shocking and illegal, considering I was a victim, and he was an officer of SAPOL. The audacity of this man. He had, what I thought was, an arrogant overconfidence. He was stalking me on some levels, which was proven in later years. Something in his eyes gained my attention for years.

I was obsessed with finding the man I refer to as my 'moon' (Travis Enmon) because of police hacking social media platforms. I was not sure whether my American was American at all. This man, who in 2014 said "their gaslighting you" Nazi style, saved my sanity. My ex-fiancée, Travis Paul Enmon (DOB16JAN1989) cock blocking the crowd, and my disinterest in a relationship or a man kept my attitude towards the SAPOL freemason interested and not interested.

Cou Cou, I nicknamed the obsessed freemason. Who deserves credit where credit is due had actually stood up justly regarding incidents stemming from police corruption that have affected my life. And is also a savage boys club player. The SAPOL officers' timing could not have been worse. I was not really interested and was being used and abused by police forces.

Sharing a kind of mutual obsession for years, a fucking weird relationship/friendship made up of interactions that were twisted and at times hateful. In 2021/2022, it was clear that this Freemason officer, who was not getting his way, had engaged in malicious and sour activities in retaliation for our out-of-control flirtation with my life, as he had been involved in maladministration and entrapment. Interacting for a decade with no physical interaction at all, really. Cou Cou was so nervous around me. When I touched his hand at the Mount Gambier Police Station one day, picking up a pen, his body language was unmistakable. He froze, time froze, yet that was the most physical we had been - a brush of skin in a moment. A man, the only man I think I've loved, with no explicit thoughts yet overbearing explicit thoughts. Psychologically, we tore each other apart, somewhat necessarily, it seemed to make us better and worse whenever we interacted.

Another notable lover that I never saw naked - rather disappointing, I nearly lived with was a metal drummer turned VICPOL cop. Seriously, these cops kept finding me, and the reasons behind their seedy interests were not good. I did actually find drummer boy cop very attractive. It was 2019, and my god watching him drumming naked would have been a dream. Unfortunately, he was just a boy who played drums and wanted to be a hero, the hero status somewhat achieved. I personally think he should have stuck to drumming. We were nothing much more than internet crushes, really, social media buddies and lovers, but it was fun. He was fun when it wasn't misunderstood conversation and petty text bickering.

♥ ○ ▽   ⊓

Liked by **marciabnoose** and **others**

Another notable person was a doctor who subtly flirted with me for months during my time in Alice Springs. Apparently, he was around 30, he told me, and he was someone I could kiss for hours - let alone the rest. I was glad when that day finally came, and I wasn't disappointed. Being the first man I had been attracted to in a few years, he followed me around the Casino bars as I worked as a bar attendant, until I thought fuck it, and gave him my number. Not my usual approach to men. Liking the audacity of the Freemasons' approach until this point in time, I had not really admired anyone else.

Taking every opportunity to stare at the doctor's gorgeous features and luxurious long hair. Feeling guilt but no remorse, as I was engaged to my ex-fiancée, with whom I had never been physical, and without a ring, I was so torn about whether or not my moon was really the one. I was literally on the verge of calling off my engagement, which is why I made the move I did, handing out my phone number. My man had been incarcerated for six months before I knew where he was, and he left many details out when explaining why he was again in jail. A pound of mushrooms I could look past as a crime, but his offences this time caused harm, and I didn't know what to do with those facts, nor how to feel. So, with the doctor I lay - I swear this moment was the lamest I had ever sexually been, until I was defeminized for five months in AWP (Political Prisoner #192703 explains that).

Back to the doctor delivering a rhythm I seriously contemplated more of - if the situation was different. Recklessly endangered and engaged were a poor combination to invite anyone into. I was so surprised by him, his interests, his manner - not just his rhythm. It killed me that I rocked up in an oversized jumper and track pants with my figure not quite perfect. I was keen to make a go of it one more time at least before he left Alice Springs! Alas, this was not to be. I then brushed off the advances he made from Tasmania when his contract took him there, ever more devastating—the guy, not marriage material, but Cute. I took the first opportunity to release his hair from the hair tie that held it, and my god, the desire to do that again was overwhelming. My self-control is beyond impressive - and probably slightly stupid considering I called my engagement off not long after sleeping with him. Wish him all the happiness in the world.

Mainly a relationship kind of girl, being single for years in my thirties was actually really nice considering I had to do my own dishes, take out my own bin, and carry my own luggage. I think I've been in love in every relationship I've ever been in and broken up with each of them with no regrets, not wanting the relationship back. I love all my friends too (we don't get freaky despite some lesbian rumours). Each to their own, but sleeping around is not my thing. I've had my fair share of fun, rejecting a list of men; I certainly have not earned the slut title, but I've had fun in life. Momentary missionary, drunk and barely remembered sex, etc, are not on my wish list of fun. Love is a natural emotion. Love, and to be sincerely loved. I must say that I do not feel that love is to suffer over and over again at the hands of anyone. A sorry said more than twice is not a mistake; it is a choice.

"A thousand half-loves must be forsaken to take one whole heart home." — Rumi.

The turbulence of life had seriously had a hold of me by the time I was thirty-five years old. I was truly happy alone with only myself to trust. Trusting only myself for most of the third decade of my life, and I actually liked it. It felt like dying while alive, to be so twisted and torn between love and life. Life won every time in this numb sense of contentment I maintained as the unignorable truth of sex offences and use of my life as rape bait overwhelmed aspirations that love was transparent. More mystical than a muse, more apparent than attraction was what I needed, if anything at all.

Most of the time, I loathed men during this period of my life. No trust, no love, and God knows I was low on trust. Relationships were too complex; they required trust and time. Two things I did not have. It seemed inappropriate to entertain the possibility that I could tolerate another failed relationship, let alone be in such a tremendously unique mode of survival. Whistleblowing on police corruption and governance, sex offenders cover-ups from 2014 onwards. I agreed to marry my American boyfriend seriously in 2021 (his third proposal) on June 11. Travis Paul Enmon, Doc No 8228, was incarcerated on the twenty-fourth of June 2021. Quoting a news report, I first read after hearing my man was incarcerated as follows: 'Having prior knowledge that Enmon has a Goose Creek address, Goose Creek Police officers have been actively searching for him," GCPD officials said.

"Hearing the 911 call that Enmon had been sighted at the Walmart Neighbourhood Market.' – LIVE 5 News WCSC By Ray Rivera;

–

Published: Jun. 24, 2021 at 3:37 PM EDT Updated: Jun. 24, 2021 at 11:41 PM EDT. I loved my American Guy, my moon, for most of these years. So, I was looking forward to meeting and marrying the man I thought would be just like me.

It was mid-2021, when he was in South Carolina, USA, and I was in Adelaide, South Australia, and we were finally dancing, we were engaged. Like the Sun and the Moon dance across the sky! Basking in the idea of a relationship and engagement. For the third time, I had agreed to marry him. When it was official, I was so happy.

Even when Travis was first incarcerated, his charges were rather fanciful – except for the offences he actually committed. And then he lied about the details, little lies, but lies. Finally confessing to numerous lies, I finally realised   I was too broken and out of trust to love anyone, and I certainly was not going to look past his dishonesty. I broke off the engagement and settled into the idea that I would never really love again. Love requires trust; I have little trust left for such things.

I had a fling in 2024 with a climber at Mount Arapiles, Victoria, called 'Titus', and started to fall in love with an interesting American not long after this, in February 2024. By the end of 2024, I did not want a relationship. I again accepted Travis Paul Enmon's marriage proposal, not caring for anyone else to be in my life, despite some firm, annoying, and borderline illegal efforts. Lover to Lover, for ten years, led back to Travis.

Chapter Six

'VICPOL and Dame Phyllis Frost Centre'

I recorded every request I made - and recorded every request ignored. I kept a daily dot-point diary of the hours and interactions with staff I had behind the Dame Phyllis Frost Centre's (DPFC) walls. Requests for properly fitting underwear (bras = crop top) - denied, phone numbers to be placed on my contact list - denied, my property list (which was extensive as I was approached by authorities at the USA airport and detained) - initially denied, hay fever tablet - denied, access to my asthma puffer - denied, access to basic property provided to other inmates

- denied.

"If a law is unjust, a man is not only right to disobey it, he is obligated to do so." —

Thomas Jefferson.

Abuse of power and process puts the administration of justice into disrepute among right-thinking people.

"An individual who breaks a law that conscience tells him is unjust, and who willingly accepts the penalty of imprisonment to arouse the conscience of the community over its injustice, is in reality expressing the highest respect for the law."

The court said I shouldn't have been there. I'm a protester, a law scholar, and an author. The case did not fit the framework of criminality. My lawyer advocated my respectful occupations.

Media protection was just enough.

HUMAN RIGHTS MATTER, the Association Laws are Not Fit for Purpose, Justice for ALL Matters.

I am FREE. You are NOT Free from the Accountability of your Corruption. Policing (and governance) in Australia at this time can be described as operating with a 'sense of impunity and no accountability – not only no accountability to the community, but no accountability to other police.'

I was falsely imprisoned as part of the perception police needed to create to use unlawful association laws against me, even though my dad, who is really associated and has buried a gun for bikers, has never been accused of such things. Even though I am not associated with this, and I do not believe this should be a law, the right to associate is a Human Right. Arrested with a ruling on maladministration resulting in a without conviction charge laid on a victim of police crime and criminal negligence, with all that I have really done to get police attention was report and call out sex offending.

Thousands of dollars of my property were damaged and stolen by

VICPOL and prison staff via G4S in St Kilda and DPFC. I reported everything via the Ombudsman Victoria and IBAC, with these departments seemingly doing little to rectify a culture of theft, dehumanisation, and institutional abuse.

VICPOL police started spreading rumours with malicious intentions, saying I was a prostitute, informant, crown witness, and dated cops, seemingly immediately throughout DPFC and on remand at G4S. Intentionally malicious statements were spread, hoping to cause grievous bodily harm to me in custody.

I have had some valueless stolen items returned, including some petty property that was not even mine. But I have not had memorabilia, valuable items, or other lost or stolen items returned. No apology and even though the tort has been acknowledged on record by a judge and evidence of the tort is with the AFP, VICPOL assigned to investigate VICPOL police sent a letter stating they required thirty-five weeks to find hundreds of dollars of perfume, replace my laptop due to damage, return stolen pearls which were New York Fashion Week garment embellishments, replace thousands of dollars of cosmetics, damaged jewellery, etc. "Justice delayed is justice denied" is a legal maxim. It means that if legal redress or equitable relief to an injured party is available but not forthcoming promptly, it is effectively the same as having no remedy at all.

This principle is the basis for the right to a speedy trial and similar rights, which are meant to expedite the legal system, because of the unfairness to the injured party who sustained the injury, having little hope for a timely and effective remedy and resolution. The phrase has become a rallying cry for legal reformers who view courts, tribunals, judges, arbitrators, administrative law judges, commissions, or governments as acting too slowly in resolving legal issues — either because the case is too complex, the existing system is too complex or overburdened, or because the issue or party in question lacks political favour. Individual cases may be affected by judicial hesitancy to make a decision. Statutes and court rules have tried to control the tendency, and judges may be subject to oversight and even discipline for persistent failures to decide matters in a timely manner or accurately report their backlog. When a court takes a matter "under advisement" – awaiting the issuance of a judicial opinion, order, or judgment and forestalling final adjudication of a lawsuit or resolution of a motion – the issue of timeliness of the decision(s) comes into play.

The Victorian courts delayed the release of the court audio to me for years, which proves irrefutably that malpractice within courthouses was being used to try to assist police with this insidious institutional abuse and conspiring. I am entitled to the record, and I am entitled to sue for false incarceration. Courts, administrations, and a judge are involved in malfeasance. A glaring and irrefutable display of a lack of separation of powers, and proof that our judicial system has been compromised by illegal conduct, bribery, and legislation that is not fit for purpose.

This chapter is not a light-hearted read. This facility was run by many creeps, pigs, and thieves dressed as its authority.

I ended up in DPFC because I reported a VICPOL police officer, Damian Ferrari, for sexual assault and domestic violence in November 2018. In 2019, from the station where Damian was a station commander, he retaliated with an illegal intervention application, which he supported with falsified claims of criminality against me. His actions should have been addressed well before August 2022, when I was falsely imprisoned. False imprisonment is an unlawful restraint of a person by another within a fixed area. The judge, on September 5th, acknowledged the offence did not fit the punishment of incarceration, that I should not have been incarcerated. Stating to the court that I would not have learned anything from the experience, as I was a protester, not a criminal. A correct assessment, therefore, from the judge, I was not a threat to the police. Nor was there any need for intervention by persons whose core mission should be public safety - to reduce and patrol crime. Furthermore, police should accept responsibility for their personal fear reduction because they are the experts on crime and disorder. A little girl who has no recorded history of physical violence against anyone, especially while protesting my right to resolution, fair trial, and safety.

Many of the 'screws' (as inmates referred to them) were ex-Victorian

Police Force (VICPOL) police officers were Corrections Officers, inmates claimed. Speaking to very few inmates as a public figure in separation, there were claims that the government facilitated and groomed children into prostitution in Victoria (a likeness to allegations made in South Australia) through the Department of Families, Fairness and Housing (DFFH). Housing young teens with older girls already in the sex industry who were providing services to police officers and government officials sworn to protect them. Taken from said abusive homes to be sold into sexual slavery. These allegations investigated would be easy to prove to be true. I was disturbed beyond words by the enormity and consistency between states regarding paedophilia and grooming young women into the sex industry via family services departments. The emotional distress I personally felt after being sexually assaulted and raped by men involved with the sex industry in numerous states over the years, since assisting a homicide investigation overseen by the Australian Federal Police (AFP), was overwhelming. The more sex industry facts I was exposed to, the more emotional distress it caused me - it was pretty unbearable.

An innocent victim, stuck in over a decade of police abusing power and process to cover up governmental department misconduct. A repetitive cover-up of SAPOL criminality, which actually spans decades regarding sex offenders. In 2022, during my efforts to resolve numerous reports against sex offenders and with tort claims against VICPOL, the police forces allowed the worst of torts to occur as a direct result of abuse of power and process. Perjury committed knowingly by Horsham Police, Victoria police, under Commissioner Shane Patton, I quote, stated they "Tow the line of VICPOL," which is not only malfeasance but making false or misleading statements while under oath that intentionally deceive the court is a felony. Since judges and juries base their decisions on witness testimonies and evidence, lying under oath can significantly harm a case. Or benefit it if the police are seeking incarceration from their false narrative, it seems. VICPOL illegally incarcerating me was assisted by ICE - Immigration USA, Border Force USA., the AFP Australia, and NSWPOL Australia.

If I was the AFP commissioner at this time witnessing the tort. The tort evident as approval to travel was given to me initially, I would have reported the police responsible for the tort via integrity avenues and refused to cooperate with torts on grounds of legal and code of conduct articles. The Code of Conduct articles state that law enforcement officials shall not commit any act of corruption. They shall also rigorously oppose and combat all such acts. Law enforcement officials shall always fulfil the duty imposed upon them by law, by serving the community and by protecting all persons against illegal acts, consistent with the high degree of responsibility required by their profession. In the performance of their duty, law enforcement officials shall respect and protect human dignity and maintain and uphold the human rights of all persons. No law enforcement official may inflict, instigate, or tolerate any act of torture or other cruel, inhuman, or degrading treatment or punishment, nor may any law enforcement official invoke superior orders or exceptional circumstances such as a state of war or a threat of war, a threat to national security, internal political instability, or any other public emergency as a justification of torture or other cruel, inhuman, or degrading treatment or punishment. Law enforcement officials shall respect the law and the present Code. They shall also, to the best of their capability, prevent and rigorously oppose any violations of them. Law enforcement officials who have reason to believe that a violation of the present Code has occurred or is about to occur shall report the matter to their superior authorities and, where necessary, to other appropriate authorities or organs vested with reviewing or remedial power. Briefly, on the legal grounds to refuse to participate in a tort, these included: irregular judgment, the term given to the judgment that is contrary to a practice of the court, and is contrary to the mode of procedure that is established. Judicial review is about **setting the boundaries of government power**. It is about ensuring government officials obey the law and act within their prescribed powers. Access to the courts for the purpose of judicial review is an important common law right.

My safety should have been paramount for years, not an assurance of harassment by paedophile protecting police. No one on this planet should spend decades combating a clear ongoing abuse of power and process - institutional harassment. As a whistle-blower (whistleblowing vulgar sex crimes) my emotional distress levels should have been as much a concern as my safety due to agendas and persons who may benefit from trying to push me to the refuge of suicide. And in my eyes, I should never have had to battle the police, so to speak, to obtain justice. Personally unless it were a public act of desperation (e.g. suicide on the AFP footsteps writing police names in blood to seek the refuge of suicide) I would not commit suicide so I would be very hard to frame in this circumstance, that said I should not have been being led by governmental and police cover ups into trying to kill myself or even have been concerned about this agenda. Rhetoric from police in conversation has apparently proven this to be the case. The false incarceration tort from VICPOL, they clearly hoped, was that straw to push me over the edge. This moment hurt, was embarrassing and pushed suicidal thoughts that I moved past upon release. As for the incarceration torts that followed in South Australia, the result of that could have been this fatal. I honestly have no respect for any of these dehumanisers and hate to think about the impacts of their negative decisions within life in general.

Spending years exposed to a corrupt and flawed justice system, suffering from its torture and the emotional distress of experiencing the whole system and its vested failures all the way to DPFC has severely increased my PTSD. After days detained at the detention centre (goal/jail) located in Honolulu, Hawaii, USA, I passed through

Mascot NSW police station custody and the corrections facility in NSW. Then spent days in G4S in Melbourne before being placed on remand in custody at DPFC. Police used irrelevant, inadmissible bail applications by SAPOL, resulting in 'Not Guilty' outcomes, to have the courts refuse bail. Damian Ferrari, at the time of his intervention application in 2019, had been reported to VICPOL for sex offending and domestic violence (DV) against me; he should have been criminally investigated as well as investigated by IBAC of Victoria, as I reported to Alyx Gray. Instead, my statement was exploited by VICPOL, with the IBAC report made by Alyx Gray and later by me, not preventing Damian Ferrari's abuse of power or resulting in him being charged at this time for DV and rape. VICPOL was allowing the malfeasance at the taxpayers' expense to be spent on years of torts engaged by a bitter, baldheaded detective in Horsham, Victoria, Mathew Olsten, who worked hard to help cover up for a VICPOL police officer guilty of domestic violence and sex offending.

Mocking up over sixty charges and numerous warrants to solidify the incarceration tort. Many other VICPOL police officers are willing to 'tow the line of VICPOL', allowing the torts to continue. Attitudes that create a divide in society, as hate breeds hate.

It was a very confronting experience being placed in DPFC. The prison environment exposed me to guards (ex-cops) stealing from

101

inmates, bullying inmates, dehumanising, sexual relations between staff and inmates, stealing money from inmate shop requests, forging inmates' signatures, medication discrepancies, and many other concerns.

The property staff and management took five (5) days to provide my extensive property list, on which nearly all items were mislisted as of poor quality, despite recent receipts proving that the items were of new quality. Many items were not listed, and upon returning my property, much of it was missing. Over three thousand ($3000.00) of damaged and stolen goods, including pages missing from my passport, which is a federal crime to deface. In Victoria, damage of this level of cost is also a criminal, not a civil offence. The police and staff involved needed to be individually charged or face criminal charges of theft. The organisatrion conspiring to mislead courts with police surrounding organized crime allegations never charged nor applicable to any case before the court should also be charged against DPFC staff.

At the time, I was engaged to American citizen Travis Paul Enmon. I had packed many items of personal and sentimental value. My luggage also included new clothing and shoes, as well as new cosmetics, perfumes, and other luxuries, to last for at least three months. I had applied in 2019 to work for the FBI, letting go of the thought that the organisation was honest after it was clear that Christopher Wray was willing to breach privacy laws (illegally, with no good

102

operational objective I could see anyway), which his predecessor James Comey was not so easily persuaded to do. Although concerned about the Integrity of the place (while in Rome), I intended to visit the FBI in New York and had contacted the office in New York via phone, simply stating that I would attend the office upon my arrival. This phone call was made in approximately March 2022, before my leaving for the planned Barbwire Noose attendance in NYFW2022 and prior to Barbwire Noose Couture featuring on the Sustainable Couture Runway, Alice Springs, NT, AUS.

DPFC is a taxpayer-funded facility, apparently built on an old rubbish dump, according to inmates' rumours. It is located outside the Melbourne CBD, having been built in 1996. It was the first privately owned prison in Victoria, but was transferred to public ownership in 2000 and is now run by Corrections Victoria. Tracey Jones has been the General Manager since 2000 and was the listed General Manager at the time I was incarcerated. She was apparently away on leave when I was reporting the abhorrent state and activities of the prison with the acting General Manager, as useless as evidently Tracey was to have created such a cesspool culture. More examples of the levels of immorality of DPFC are in the facts that a male claiming he is female (yet has a penis) has raped (and been allowed by staff inmates stated) incarcerated women in the facility like a pet to use and abuse; another example is an ICE addict groomer who was a priority in the facility as her regular incarceration allowed staff to harass inmates using her while she flashed her flat chest at staff during count. There are plenty more examples there that show this facility is psychologically fucked, like a woman who murdered children with a garden tool, who uses garden tools daily. Paedophiles making kids' toys for their rooms, inmates, etc. The place is not a rehabilitation unit, nor will you come out of that shithole better for society. To me, DPFC was creating career criminals, showing little remorse in their dehumanisation and no real avenues to assimilate back into society. On face value, the facility appears maintained. Once you're on the inside, you realize the prison is essentially just a gang of ex-cops and guards, bitter about life, who prioritize their own best interests above all else.

Before my incarceration in 2021, the facility flagged a specific area of focus. It was apparently intended to address the ongoing problematic workplace culture issues and practices that discourage the reporting of suspected corrupt conduct. Clearly not the real focus, just public fodder, the acting general manager, while I was imprisoned, blatantly covered up maladministration and criminal conduct where my signature was forged. Signature forgery offence is a fraud offence, and the penalties can be severe, including imprisonment. My signature was forged on a shop purchase document dated August 29, 2022, while I was detained in the Swan Two unit – also known as 'the slots'. Staff, without worry of repercussions, committed fraud and

misappropriated funds, stating they were justified in committing signature fraud as I was in jail. The purchase total with my shopping list choices modified by staff even exceeded my original order; the fraudulent malpractice was theft of my finances, also. The Swan two-unit at this time was a disgusting unit with the bare minimum provided. You are apparently locked up here as a disciplinary action. A cycle of doing the wrong thing by staff going unpunished, trying to change those imprisoned, is ironic. Evidently, the unit where dodgy guards sent prisoners who knew their rights, used phone time to call IBAC and wrote to the ombudsman, as this was the reason for my visit to the slots of DPFC for a few days before being allocated to protection due to media interest and my role as a crown witness. I was starved for eighteen hours of the day in this unit, given less food, and was not really given out-of-cell time. My dietary requirements went unmet, and I was given meat meals even when my orders were vegetarian.

The facts of this offence are irrefutable. I was shown a photocopy of the rewritten and falsified document by a female staffer to whom I reported the malfeasance on the 30th of September 2022. Just after a senior staff member, Mr Ramsey, had visited me and apologised for numerous concerns I raised regarding my property, hygiene, nutrition, dehumanising behaviour, and safety. And just before the guards stated I have no rights and needed to realise I was in prison at their criminal whims.

The culture of DPFC, from what I witnessed, was that at least thirty to fifty percent of the staff who interacted with me were complicit or had engaged in misconduct against civil rights and/or of a criminal nature. As a crown witness, I can commend the facility regarding the separation of myself from mainstream, initiated by Brian Hinkley. This was a responsible decision and did keep me from some of the dangers surrounding being falsely incarcerated. Unfortunately, the facility, via Joy McDonald and other vindictive staff, was told of my crown witness status, which in turn made interactions with inmates quickly become questionable. All of this is mainly motivated by the seedy old staff's power trip. Some are seemingly trying to blame biker groups for the harassment, even though bikers have never threatened my life. The jail, which served as a regular stay off the streets for some, did manage to convince a couple of career criminals to be willing to engage in petty behaviours, including trying to incite fighting.

The correctional officers and rules favoured some of the vilest offenders. Paedophiles and child murderers were provided with the same tools they used for murder to garden recreationally, paedos given wool to make kids toys - it was a sick psychological shit haven. Literally a shit haven. Groomers and ICE addicts flirted with guards and were rewarded for fraternising.

There were six of us in the Elliot unit during my forced stay there. Two of the five other women tried to slag off and shit stir, yet they were not willing to take it further. Leading up to my court date for release, the harassment increased. I recall one of them telling me I would be beaten in mainstream, to which I replied Are you threatening me, My PTSD finally snapped at her after too much of her niggling. She responded to no. She is on the couch, and I am sitting on the kitchen bench next to the knives. A smart answer, considering I felt threatened by her threatening body language, which is clearly recorded on the cameras as the incident unfolded in the living area of this unit. Out of a group of six girls, some of the behaviour was 'putrid' as described by others, with me having no prior comparison for the behaviours. Knickers were making their way into a kitchen cupboard within days of being present in this shared environment, and the psychological games between inmates were in full swing. A girl incarcerated stated the knickers were a replica of a photograph in her phone, believing the stunt was directed at her. One regular ICE addict piece of scum tried to crack onto me, clearly not realising I won't be converted from the dick – don't fucking touch me. I swear to God, if this shit had gotten too hairy in DPFC, this abuse of power and process, false incarceration, would have ended in the loss of a life. I was more than prepared to shove a pen in the neck of anyone who started to stray from their lane.

Elliot unit was a newly opened old COVID unit, the protection unit to which I was assigned on remand, and the last unit I had seen before VICPOL withdrew over fifty trumped-up charges, and I was found 'Not Guilty'—slapped with a fine for VICPOL's abuse of the justice system on the fifth of September 2022. DPFC took six hours to process the forms and left me to pay nearly one hundred dollars for a taxi to the hotel, where I would reside until I was back in the safety of my vehicle and under a roof - necessities I did not have in the state of Victoria.

Being held at DPFC was a traumatic experience enough without further exposures to police aiding and abetting - complicity and common purpose regarding the commission of an offence, sex crimes. The emotional distress from victimisation by many staffers of DPFC, plus being exposed to further trauma, had me released from false imprisonment, completely traumatised. Breaking down in the taxi that transported me to the emergency house, I would reside in until I was able to return to my home state of South Australia.

Torts, the abuse of power and process by VICPOL, a cover-up of sex offenders, was what saw me dragged across countries and states of Australia to DPFC. The experience was so traumatic that it took over a day for me to play music, my usual pastime, and months to feel normal and clean.

Having firsthand witnessed the destructiveness of Abuse of Power and Process, I firmly believe that, above all, Liberty and Humanity (Human Rights Law) must dominate legislation and politics. As we enter the exclusive and boundless possibilities of a digital age, we must embrace individualism and morality with grace. The rejection of academic advice provided to the Parliament of Australia in 2008 regarding the South Australian Government of Mike Rann and the Serious Organised Crime Act 2008 is the perfect example of ideals over morality, over Human Rights. Governments given the power to deprive the rights of others have irrefutably proven to be using the legislation in tyranny against the Australian people – a draconian law implemented by tyrants. The rights and justice for all are something that needs protecting – relentlessly. I am a strong advocate against dehumanisation and for a Bill of Rights Australia. Dedicated to always advocating for a humane society.

NOTE: The five odd months spent in Adelaide Women's Prison (AWP) for incarceration torts, as mentioned, are described in Political Prisoner #192703 – The Price of Unlawful Enforcement, an International publication.

Chapter Seven

'Poetry'

Poems by yours truly.

OBLIVION

Can you feel me now? As time is paralysed.

The hollowness of my eyes, The Truth behind your lies.

Death is not but something we do once, But many times in life,
before the body dies.

Choked and broken, Butchered and bent.

Can you feel that piece of you?

The lost piece you sent. But a thousand miles, And a thousand
times.

The back and forth of lust, Obnoxious venom in spite. Oceans
could not tear us apart,

Intertwined, a modern Bonnie and Clyde.

Can you feel me now, my darling? While we're at our most distant.

Our most broken, Our most torn.

Our most existent in this circumstantial existence, Our Love.

Our Spite,

The delight in the night.

The unchannelled emotions, Turbulence in flight.

The irreparable repair, Unattainable separation.

Harmonious differentiation, Oblivion in elation.

Written for my Moon, born in the USA.

Marcia BNoose Saturday 31st July 2021

Le Droit Humain Lodge 406

AUSTRALIA

When the Moon met the Sun.

You dazzled the night, Shining so bright in the sunlight.

That twinkle and shine, You look So divine.

Amongst the clouds in the sky, The lies and the highs.

You were by my side, Until one night.

We met – you and I.

Our spark igniting night into day, And day to night.

Locked in a gaze, The sky was a haze.

Segments of erupting desire,

The shape shifting moon will never tire.

My light will never burn out, It was the doubt.

As you and I stood side by side, But you lied.

You said you'd stay,

But you moved away. After our sweet embrace,

You passed over me in a day.

To romance the night with your light, As I bring the day to light.

In love and lust - I decided to run, When the Moon met the Sun.

AUSTRALIA

Marcia Anita Hobbs (1984), 31 March 2020.

INFINITY

That shallow Never mellow. Turn to jello.

Every time I see you kind of love.

That can't live without you. I will never doubt you.

Touch my soul, chaotic kind of love.

That superficial Totally iconic Unforgettable

Twisted and regrettable kind of love.

That you And me

Us only to be. Death defying Universal

Uncontrollably Undeniable Kind of love. That mystifying.

Lust for life Get into strife.

Kisses for nothing Sex on Sunday

Every day's a fun day Inconceivable Totally believable Choke on

cream Make you scream.

Die together kind of love. That nothing is everything And everything is

nothing.

Full of mistakes Everything breaks.

Censored kind of love.

Written about Love for Love. Read – literally off paper. I was a bit
boring actually, at Alice Springs Poetry Fest 2022. See Love, Be Love,
We Are Love. Marcia Anita Hobbs (1984), 20 June 2020

The Intertwine

It is within alchemy that we can feed the most intenseness of our soul. The essence of unity beyond words and time the ultimate elation, sex. When you and I combine in exploration of every element of sensation to engage ourselves into an art of erotic love making, desire so intense it is fed by universal energy blinding our lives to forever intertwine. "Love is magic my dear" it whispers, "yet it's not what you seek in another but what you seek in yourself. He is the key to the light, you are the door that needs NO key to open, SHINE." - Marcia Anita Hobbs

30/11/18

The Sky

The moon takes many forms, Phases – like life,

Though None as fine as yours. As the dawn rose this day,

We lingered,

Light – mine and yours for a cause.

Never truly able to run, Whenever the moon meets the sun.

Entwined every night, Dancing in a forever cabaret. This
distance so bright,

This romance – so inept. Eclipses of beauty, Delivered like duty.

A sun and a moon like no other in this universe, Obsessed in orbit.

I rise and set,

You follow, then disappear. Knowing I will always be there.

For the red of my heart, Is the heat in the dark night.

Your phase of black and white, Energy casting delight.

If I burn out, We all die.

The blue-sky care not,

The trees, the frogs, the wildlife of life.

Our Wild life.

The divine sky is yours,

And we are entrenched night and day.

Our bed of clouds, Gaps where we lay.

Whether it's your star,

Or Mine.

Forever we shine, In every cycle.

In ever-changing times,

It's always you and I.

Until I turn cold,

Dark and distant like you.

I will light your world my love, And you,

You will always be my ecstasy.

A muse so powerful in Destiny, That we can achieve anything.

Side by side, Or miles apart.

Love is what we are here for,

To be Love, To find Love,

To cherish Love, To die Love.

Forever entwined – your atoms and mine

05/07/2021

Marcia Anita Hobbs

HOW TRAGIC

And so I provoked you,

Like no other stirring your insides with unintentional intent.

You consume me,

Every empty vessel within my skin, In holding of nothing.

Absence a delusional illusion,

The game does not stop and I will not falter. For as we pass the phase of unwanted change,

It betters you.

And that betters me, Though hindered in growth,

We bloom.

He said you were losing,

All I seen is you all at a loss.

To live and die, And cheat and lie,

At any cost. Total demise,

No compromise.

How tragic.

06/01/2019 Marcia Anita Hobbs Lodge 406, Adelaide, South Australia.

Cowards Crave Comfort

Does it dissolve, Like church bread on Sunday.

That bland idealisation, Of the world in anticipation.

Marcia Anita Hobbs, 1984.

And in the absence of Fear, it is not only ourselves we find, but life
and death themselves.

Marcia Anita Hobbs,

23/03/16

Untitled No words, No Poems, Just Love.

Subsiding further into this reclusive radiance,

It feels so natural, The sweet essence of nothing among the
unknown,

What is stagnant in emotion, Floods my inner core,

Revelation of Nothing within this dark sorrow,

Yet Everything among the night, It grows fonder yet weak,

Weeping eyes under the moonlight.

I feel you, Yet I don't see you.

I'm not in a place of longingly,

Only a place of peace, Searching for your absence,

Has brought me too my knees. Love is not the gift of life, But the
giving of a life,

An atrocity of devastation. Has us with no destination.

Empty words paint a notion, With meanings vaster than the ocean.

Anonymously they breath,

Truth to your emotion.

Falling now, Substantial and unsustained. Maybe they are Right

119

baby.

Intimacy they can't explain,

Just contain.

19/12/2018, Marcia Anita Hobbs Lodge 406, Adelaide, South Australia

Always remember that the evil Wants You to dwell on your mistakes. – Marcia Anita Hobbs, Lodge 406.

Chapter Eight

'Study'

Never Stop Learning. No one knows everything, and you never know enough.

I have studied for most of my life, not just the conventional schooling up to year twelve, or the compulsory studies required for work. I study for life, in areas to help me grow and thrive. Starting childcare studies around twenty years of age for motherhood - lucky for me, this study also benefited my swim teaching, as I have no kids. One of the many reasons why I have time to write autobiographies about my life is a blessing. I'm not one to have children out of wedlock, at this rate, I may not have children at all *giggles*. I am glad I didn't waste too much energy on these studies in the end. Not married, heading to forty with no children – society says tragic, I say I'm not a divorce statistic.

Legal studies were the study I deferred upon leaving school. In 2021, I began the process of revisiting my longing desire to study law and become a lawyer.

Some functional studies I have undertaken for life are in accounting. I hold a Certificate IV in Accounting, and I plan to complete the diploma in the future. Accounting Studies is something that can benefit anyone, I believe. Being savvy with your money is a great trait, really. Real Estate studies have been handy, even though I hated the job.

When I entered the world of entrepreneurship with my brand, Barbwire Noose®, I completed a Certificate IV in Small Business. This type of study, I think, is beneficial for anyone in a small business. Taking on your own venture, you can never have too much knowledge regarding trade, forms, business processes, proposals, and much more.

Completing a master's in business administration while reporting sexual trauma and numerous acts of sexual abuse is something I wouldn't advise. The course is taking me years to complete due to the cover-ups engaged by the police force, desperate to bury the truth of a police force harbouring many sex offenders. A most unpleasant experience made even more unpleasant when having to postpone studies due to the emotional distress and torturous trauma. The negative external factors do not detract from the value of the study; this course provides a solid educational foundation for starting a company, which is essential for my brand, Barbwire Noose. Yet, the psychological impacts of the cover-up torts and ongoing effects affected many of my studies until they were resolved.

Historical studies, though not formal avenues, have always fascinated me. Indulging in the evolution of humanity from the Egyptians, through the Kings and Queens, to today's society provides an objective perspective on our societal development.

Documentaries, studies, and media platforms provide broad subject content. An understanding of how and why things are as they are, along with insights into the what, how, and when, makes it more straightforward for me to comprehend the establishment of cultures, freedoms, Democracy, and Politics. Politics is my future ambition. The Magna Carta of 1215 is one of the most significant documents in human history, representing a milestone in the pursuit of freedom for the people—the bible, a foundation of belief and controversy globally. The pyramids fascinate people to this day about how they were truly established. Aliens fascinate me; there's no way in the universe that we are alone or the sole existing species in our galaxy. These are all topics that capture my attention and spare time.

Human Rights, to me, are the ultimate foundation of a democratic society and are the essential basis for legislation. I engage in online studies of any rights-related topics and literature wherever possible. I try to keep up to date with developments and decisions made by the United Nations. Without reciting everything that is out there, I like to think that, thus far, I have engaged in meaningful learning about civilization, common law, and natural law. I will continue to learn more in the future—believing strongly that the Universal Declaration of Human Rights is fundamental to just laws, peace, and civil society.

I study areas of interest and towards employment. For education and personal development.

Diversely, I have studied suicide prevention and hold knowledge about crisis counselling, courses stemming from volunteer work. Undertaking a First Aid course at high school is a qualification required to be a swim teacher. It is a course that requires refreshing after a specific period of time and is a qualification I think I'll continue for the rest of my life, at least in service to myself, my peers, and the broader community. Mandatory reporting is also a course of study I required as a teacher, obtaining it specifically to teach. The course helps you recognise family abuse and is compulsory for teachers.

Lifeline e-Learning Completion Certificate

This is to certify that

Marcia Hobbs

has completed the course

CS Non-Suicidal Self Injury (NSSI) PD 2018

25 January 2018

Course Grade: 100.00 %

Issued by Lifeline Australia

To date, I have also studied Music Production, Sustainable Fashion, Policy and Governance, Hospitality, and Gambling. I will never stop learning.

Life is learning. Don't hold yourself back; take every opportunity to feed your amazing mind, learn, and try something new. Always be creative and innovative. Idle hands are the devil's work.

YouTube is a Great teacher, too. Dear Reader, Never stop learning.

Chapter Nine

'Volunteering'

The most significant achievements I have made in life have not been on a payroll.

Time is precious; if you give it away for free, make sure it's worthwhile. Volunteering is a dignified dedication; if it doesn't feel dignified, you probably shouldn't dedicate your free time to it.

I volunteered for a job as a Swim Teacher, having taught aquatics for most of my life and also given my time to older people, Lifeline, political parties, animal charities, and community events, to name a few. All voluntary experiences equally rewarding, though some of these voluntary roles are rather challenging. It's important that when giving your time that you have left enough time for yourself, self-care, personal and social responsibilities.

Volunteering at an aged care facility while unemployed in 2002. After volunteering in aged care, I realised that the empathetic nature of the work was healing, much like the way the company of pets heals people.

In 2017, the University of Sydney, to celebrate National Volunteer Week, spoke to some University experts in happiness, psychology, and pharmacology to find out the real benefits of volunteering. Here are some of the findings: People who "give" – either money or their time – have been reported to be happier and healthier than those who don't. A 2007 study led by Arthur Brooks of Syracuse University found that givers were forty-two percent more likely than non-givers to say they were "very happy".

Dr. Rebecca Pinkus, Lecturer in Psychological Statistics, adds, "Volunteering keeps you in a positive mood and can help lift you out of a negative mood."

The study goes on to say…..

' There's a bit of a catch-22 when it comes to volunteering – we can't just volunteer to get the benefits. It's a lot like how you can't just demand that you'll be happy on the spot.

To get the full benefits of volunteering, the trick is to get involved in something you're passionate about. This is precisely what the former President of the University's Alumni Council, Peter Shaw (BSc '89 LLB(Hons) '91 MBA(Exec)

'05) did when he took on the voluntary role. "There is something about giving to others that adds enjoyment to life. Finding the organisation or cause that engages your heart and mind, and contributing to it in ways that are meaningful to you and valuable to others, is a great gift to uncover," says Mr. Shaw.

Volunteering can also be a great way of increasing purpose, especially in retirement.

So go, get out there and find something you're passionate about, and feel better knowing you've helped others. I absolutely *love* this and believe it is one hundred percent true. Volunteering also can make you happier and is beneficial for your health, so why wouldn't you Get Involved?

Chapter Ten

'Freemasonry'

"The source of every crime is some defect of the understanding, or some error in reasoning, or some sudden force of the passions. Defect in the understanding is ignorance; in reasoning, erroneous opinion." - Thomas Hobbes, Leviathan.

Freemasonry is in my life a cult that found me and, bluntly, is one of the greatest and damaging good vs evil regimes outside of Nazi war times.

To be one, ask one - the first mistake as motive overshadows the best of freemasons.

Greed, power, lust, delusional belief, and manipulation are not the basis of Freemasonry, but it is the basis for the blind to lead the blind. For years, I suffered the greed, power, and lust that compromised a society built on morality. The disconnect between what was said and what was done led me to resign from Lodge 406 in 2019. By 2021, the desire to return to this lodge was almost non- existent, yet my desire to contribute to the good I believed freemasons are overruled the irrational thought that a bad apple ruins the bunch.

"A peculiar system of morality, veiled in allegory and illustrated by symbols". – This is Freemasonry. For those unaware, the mark of a real freemason is in his 'moral' actions, not his hand signals, jewellery, or stance. Those men are the hated boys' club. I understand your detest if that's how you feel. I honestly think the same way about Freemasonry's bigotry and deceit.

I entered Freemasonry keen as mustard in 2015 after enquiring. I was happy to be accepted into a religion I felt I really connected with—more than Christianity or other beliefs. I was excited to be surrounded by like-minded peers and found peace in the old customs and symbolism. I love everything about Freemasonry

except the greed of man and its uncontrollable lust for power. Co-Freemasonry is filled with much less innuendo than the commonly known male-only Freemasonry.

▲ ▲ ▲

Blessed Humanity Be

Sister Marcia Hobbs, Adelaide Lodge No. 406

With a heart of light,
And soul of purity
Cleansed free of sin,
Gracing humanity.

Rough in cut,
Smooth by nothing less
Than humanity's progress
And his forever caress.

Careful in flight,
With no fear of the night.
The moon shining right,
With the sun always in sight.

▲ ▲ ▲

Reading esoteric literature and being surrounded by people who love poetry was delightful. As I became more estranged from my family, Freemasonry felt like family. The timing of my joining and initiation was impeccable. The rituals are performed at certain times and on specific dates. The energy of these meetings is very peaceful in ceremonies. Outside of the rituals, when it was time to be social at supper, the ugliness of the cult came about. Psychological warfare is a crime in many countries, the Freemasons, like the Catholics, CIA, global governments, militaries, etc. All engage in terrorist like tactics to save face. It was when this started to occur that I stopped trusting Freemasons on face value.

Taught the same fundamental truth, a freemason is actually expected to: walk the middle path (on the level), live a moral life (by the plumb), and do unto others as you would have them do unto you (on the square). Yes, you read that correctly. If that's not your experience, then that person needs to work on themselves before bragging about being a Freemason.

Evidently, he's also setting the example of how you should treat the jerk back

according to the belief system.

Brotherly Love

Every true Freemason will show tolerance and respect for the opinions of others and behave with kindness and understanding to their fellow creatures.

Relief

Freemasons are taught to practice charity and to care not only for their own but also for the community as a whole, both through charitable giving and voluntary efforts and works as individuals.

Truth

Freemasons strive for truth, requiring high moral standards and aiming to achieve them in their own lives. Freemasons believe that these principles represent a way of achieving higher standards in life.

This literature perfectly encapsulates the principles of a Freemason.

A Freemason should be focused on building themself as persons of integrity. Membership in a Lodge provides the structure to help achieve that goal. Being a Freemason should give members a sense of purpose, be supportive, and guide them on their life's journey.

Freemasonry, aka Masonry, refers to fraternal organisations that trace their origins to the local guilds of stonemasons and their interaction with authorities and clients. A frat it is for sure, but some of the old history dates documented have me not speculating. The symbolism is all ages, so the origins are something like that.

Here is an Australia-relevant old fact: Freemasonry has been associated with the British discovery and settlement of Australia from the very beginning.

Chapter Eleven

'Opinions and Random Shit'

Opinions are like assholes, everyone's got one - these are mine. Plus, Anything but Ordinary random shit.

The 'Princess' title. It's heritage, Indian Royalty with British history descent, also the title is real, and in terms of defamation, it really adds up to a lot of damages to call Royalty a 'sex industry worker' in malicious accusations with no basis or facts.

When a honeybee stings a mammal, its barbed stinger lodges in the skin, and the honeybee cannot remove it. Instead, it leaves the double lancet behind, along with part of its digestive tract, muscles, and nerves. This abdominal rupture is what kills the bee. I was stung by a bee during my High School years. I was riding home from the bus stop to the family farm. I swear this bee was suicidal. This bee could have flown anywhere around me this day. There were no obstructions on either side of me for at least twenty metres anyway, yet this bee chose to fly straight into me, stinging me under the chin. I looked like Jabba the Hutt with a double chin for a few days, while that bee got his wish and died from his ruptured abdomen.

My family moved to three places across South Australia by the time I was six years old. After settling in Mount Gambier, I attended four schools, including high school. Five total - four Primary Schools. I attended a primary school in Port Augusta and a Kindergarten before moving to Mount Gambier.

When it came to high school, I actually wanted to attend the city's largest high school, Mount Gambier High School, with my Middle School buddies from Primary School. But my parents chose the farming high school allocated by the government. The school with the least broad curriculum and online studies was required for advanced study. I studied two subjects online to qualify for university. By year ten, my parents wanted me to attend Mount Gambier High School, as my brother had been suspended from the allocated country school for fighting numerous times. I refused to change schools, was popular among my peers, and was at the top of the class, recording A+ and High Distinction Grades. I refused to move schools just because my brother was a fuck up. My parents only just accepted this, and are almost willing to disrupt my learning for no good reason at all. They made the best decision considering my feelings, and I stayed where I was to complete my studies.

The fact is that if we were all homosexual, the human race would be extinct. Please ponder this when you tell me that children should be brainwashed in primary school, that their gender is not relevant.

I recall this mega crazy moment when I lived at the house I rented, located on Wehl Street near Vansittart Park (Mount Gambier), when I was creating <u>Barbwire Noose</u>. I arrived at the rental premises one evening to find someone in the house. An intruder had gained entry with a key, as there was no evidence of a break-in, and all windows were secure. I was quickly running inside to grab a CD to listen to while we cruised around. I ran out of the house this evening and told my music-loving company, who was waiting in the car, that there was someone behind my bedroom door who had not broken in. A wimp, he did not want to re-enter the property with me and confront the intruder, so I did not go back in. I had pushed the bedroom door when grabbing the CD, which should have hit the wall, but it did not. The intruder I knew was behind the door. When I was dropped off back home after a few hours, nothing was stolen, and nothing seemed to have been touched.

I hold World Records. Yep, that's a fact. My first <u>Guinness World Records ™ Official</u> Attempt saw me participate with users as we undertook an online environmental sustainability lesson in 24 hours. Officially for 'The most users to take an online environmental sustainability lesson in 24 hours'. Obsessed with the stars, learning, and sustainability, this world record was for me! Winter Solstice, The Southern Hemisphere World Record Count Attempt counted the stars in the Southern Cross after a Very Insightful Lesson on Global Artificial Light, its impact, and Sustainability! Two World Records achieved thus far– I would have three but I didn't show up for one, which I don't really recall, but was some fitness challenge/achievement-oriented record – heart was NOT in that! My second World Record contribution is a Global Talkathon, a Magical World Record in the ABCD International Speakathon Event on Magical Date 11-11-2022.

I think that being objectified as a survivor of a sexual crime has been the most conflicting emotional roller-coaster of my life. The expectations of models and modelling work are at a whole new level when your mind wants to deter creeps, yet you're demanded to parade yourself around in a manner where you're supposed to be ogled and objectified.

'Objectification theory proposes that sexualisation in mass media is a primary source of objectification of women, that is, that sexualisation causes people to objectify them (i.e., to appraise them as bodies and sexual body parts and behave toward them as if they were objects; Fredrickson C Roberts, 1997)'

The first time I said 'I love you too' to a boyfriend was in year 4, in the classroom library. My first kiss was actually in the boot of a car.

On one of our first dates with my first serious boyfriend, with whom I had moved out of my home, we pulled up outside the swimming pool where I taught. I was unaware that a sign pole was directly at the car door, my guy of the time was also unaware of the sign. I got out of the car and walked straight into a pole. Such an embarrassing teen date moment was made more awkward by the apologies and reliving the moment on our next date.

Racism. It sucks. What also sucks is being ethnic and white. It is a weird racism that you face and gives appreciation to both sides of racism. If we all appreciate our differences, cultures, and nurture ourselves, our heritage, and our country, there would be no racism. We all bleed red. The bottom line is, there is dark skin and light skin; I'm white until I tan. Then I look First Nations and I *Love* that! It makes no difference, and really, we all know this. Upping your level of respect and care amongst your fellow humans is where it's at. It's on us to respect and nurture individualism, inclusive of all demographics.

I won't have a child out of wedlock - and I won't marry a twat. Hence, I was without children and unmarried in my thirties. Death is Inevitable, the Rest is Choice. Choose to dump him if he's no good; never settle for second best.

That massive marijuana bud that went missing. I took that! The pride and joy of one of my parents grow years. They left a note on the spiral staircase, stating that a camera was installed there after this golden gift from God went missing. The camera claim I didn't buy into, if there were, I would have been in trouble - my parents were very consistent at dishing out discipline. That said, they definitely noticed when the big bud went missing.

The first time I seriously considered Botox was in my thirties, unnatural, it was kind of something I wasn't keen on. Less keen on wrinkles, I went under the needle. A few friends and every beautician out still alive from years of Botox abuse, I felt it was a safe enough option for getting older. Fuck pumping my face with Botox in my twenties, the pressures and expectations of society have not changed as I've aged for women. I feel sorry for young women in this regard. That said, the abilities these days to keep physical appearances sharp (if you care) are excellent. The natural look tread is also refreshing. Just before I had the Botox, I had laser hair removal, which I purchased a home laser for to treat my legs, etc. The chick at the beautician discussed all the 20-year-olds who had Botox and had treatments herself, making the process seem very trustworthy. Unlike her work, I'm talking about laser hair removal, which involves possibly shaving off five stand-out hairs on my face and lasering them. I swear to God if Cheech's moustache had grown back, I would have been jailed for a reason (jokes).

The ex-backpacker's hostel, which had been purchased and turned into room rentals, pursued making me homeless when I was recklessly endangered in Alice Springs, and it was not pretty. The place with the KFC landlord discussed earlier. The bathroom lacked a bit of hygiene, and I'd watched my fellow renters fail to wash their hands one too many times, so I was hesitant to touch everything. Most of the time, I made it in and out of the loo without needing to shut the door—most of the time.

There was one time when a girl tiptoed into the bathroom. Like, seriously, don't sneak around shared toilets, it's weird, and there is no warning that you're coming through two doors for this bathroom.

139

Seriously, it had to be the worst time too, contemplate for a minute at what moment you would like to be caught if you were taking a bog. Would it be with your face screwed up, snapping it off? I rate this as preference two. Would it be in the moment when you're wiping with your hand behind your back, but up your crack? I rate this as preference 1. Would it be when you're closest to your shit, checking if the toilet paper is clean yet? I rate this as preference three. Preference one being the most preferred moment being caught taking a bog, unfortunately for me, I was walked in on with the door open during preference three. This stranger embarrassingly got to check if I could stop wiping yet. Meanwhile, these residents knew the importance of toilet paper. They had broken into the supply cabinet as the toilet paper was often run out, and were scolded but not asked to leave their rental. It was not until other residents complained about them that their lease was abruptly terminated.

I've fainted twice in two years due to stress. The first incident in 2021 gave me a concussion for a week. The second time was after I was released from DPFC and was witnessed by a family at a service station. Shocking everyone with the fall, the fact that my body shut down twice as police tried desperately to make me homeless shows the detrimental effects of police abuses and the severe effects psychological warfare has had on my health.

I worked at Alice Springs casino for the better part of 2022 while whistleblowing sex crimes in governance, much of the offending being

140

covered up was police and politicians using children as prostitutes. I think the casino scene was the weirdest and dodgiest environment I have ever worked in, and I also worked in Real Estate at Mount Gambier in 2009/2010 – you see some extraordinary things in people's houses. Real Estate is a lot like car sales.

All walks of life attended the casino, and I had fun serving and even occasionally having a drink with tourists and locals alike. It was mainly the environment of this place, which was fucked, filled with migrant employees and many struggles daily to keep staff at one of Australia's most famous casinos. The casino where the movie The Adventures of Priscilla, Queen of the Desert was filmed. In a place filled with history, I saw mainly drunk cops and a cover-up of a gay man's sexual offence in the casino restaurant 'Juicy Rump' toilets. The victim and offender were both employees at the casino when the crime was committed. The victim voiced his interest in homosexuality, and the offender was a stocky, openly homosexual man. The setting was a staff event, and it's here that things get weird. The victim was pushed out of work, and the offender, who openly dealt drugs at the casino, and I was told gave sexually arousing drugs to staffers, was kept in employment. When I started work, the sex offender paraded about proudly, eating at the Juicy Rump restaurant regularly. Staffers were proudly friends with their said drug dealer.

In the casino's offence case, there is evidence of sexual assault given to medical staff and the police; these facts made the environment as

141

distasteful as the crime. To make it even weirder, the victim was the child of an Australian Federal Police (AFP) force member. The police officer's family industry is "massage". At this point, facts becoming known, as an experienced police corruption whistle- blower, I thought it was apparent why he was unable to pursue a police charge of misconduct. Knowing he was involved with the police and what they are involved with and compromised by at this time. Similarly, the gay community of Alice Springs, which heavily dominates the cocaine trade, knows too. I personally was offered the drug numerous times and refused. I have never consumed cocaine and was not going to take offers from users and abusers at my workplace. The weirdest facts stated that the casino wanted the offence hush-hush, and according to police, the AFP member was embarrassed about his son's homosexual interests. It seemed that, despite the incident involving many staff members at the staff event and numerous witnesses to the two men exiting the bathroom in a completely different manner than they had entered the room, no one wanted the truthfulness of the incident to be widely reported to obtain justice. I literally watched the insidious, disgraceful attitudes I was whistleblowing in the police force in a sexual cover-up, surrounding myself in employment, a police officer associated offence and cover-up to boot—such a weird, surreal experience.

Finishing this chapter with the fact that Anything But Ordinary is not just the title of this autobiographical series. It is the eighth track on Avril

Lavigne's debut album, Let Go, released in 2002. It was written by Avril Lavigne, Lauren Christy, Scott Alspach, and Graham Edwards. I was Absolutely in *Love* with this.

The album, when it came out, and still today. This Song is my Favourite Song on the album. Often referenced as like Avril myself in my late teens and early 20s - it is a touch odd the assumption that songs and social life define people. Anyway, there is your brief explanation of the book title, and here are the lyrics too.

'Sometimes I get so weird I even freak myself out
I laugh myself to sleep It's my lullaby Sometimes I drive so fast Just to feel the danger
I want to scream
It makes me feel alive

CHORUS: Is it enough to love? Is it enough to breathe?
Somebody rip my heart out And leave me here to bleed Is it enough to die?
Somebody save my life
I'd rather be anything but ordinary please

To walk within the lines Would make my life so boring I want to know that I Have been to the extreme
So knock me off my feet Come on now give it to me Anything to make me feel alive

Is it enough to love?

Is it enough to breath?

Somebody rip my heart out And leave me here to bleed Is it enough to die?
Somebody save my life

I'd rather be anything but ordinary please I'd rather be anything but ordinary please

Let down your defences Use no common sense If you look you will see
That this world is a beautiful Accident turbulent succulent Opulent permanent, no
way
I want to taste it

Don't want to waste it away

Sometimes I get so weird I even freak myself out
I laugh my self to sleep It's my lullaby

CHORUS

Is it enough?

Is it enough to die? Somebody save my life.

I'd rather be anything but ordinary please I'd rather be anything but ordinary please

Avril Lavigne's song Anything but Ordinary from her debut album

Let Go.

LINKS

Socials:

https://www.youtube.com/@Barbwirenoose

https://au.linkedin.com/company/barbwire-noose

https://www.instagram.com/marciabnoose

https://www.instagram.com/barbwirenoose

https://www.facebook.com/BarbwireNoose/

https://mobile.twitter.com/marciabnoose/

https://mobile.twitter.com/barbwirenoose/

Websites:

https://www.marciabnoose.com/

https://www.barbwirenoose.com/

https://www.uglyheros.com.au/marcia-anita-hobbs

https://www.australianfreedomparty.com/

Publications:

Search: **Marcia Anita Hobbs** *and* **Marcia BNoose** *for publications available via state, national libraries, and leading bookstores:*

https://trove.nla.gov.au/search/advanced/category/books?creator=marcia%20anita%20hobbs

Local – Australia and International interviews and articles:

https://www.brainzmagazine.com/.../barbwire-noose-by...

https://www.brainzmagazine.com/.../empowering-daily...

https://www.brainzmagazine.com/.../secrets-from-the-eco...

https://www.brainzmagazine.com/.../spring-is-almost-over...

https://www.brainzmagazine.com/.../political-prisoner...

https://www.brainzmagazine.com/.../how-to-become-a...

https://issuu.com/lifestyle1media/docs/lifestyle_1_issue_696

https://read.amazon.com.au/?ref_=dbs_p_ebk_r00_pbcb_rnv
c00C_encoding=UTF8Casin=B08XJYTGLB

https://borderwatch.com.au/local-news/2018/01/06/lakeswim-lessons-begin/

https://borderwatch.com.au/features/2017/11/21/localfashion-designer-takes- eco-fashion-week/

ANYTHING BUT ORDINARY –

JUDGMENT AND PERCEPTION HAVE NO VALUE HERE.

BOOKNO.2

CHAPTERS

THE REBELLION

"Here's to the crazy ones. The misfits. The rebels. The troublemakers. The round pegs in the square holes. The ones who see things differently. They're not fond of rules. And they have no respect for the status quo. You can quote them, disagree with them, glorify or vilify them. About the only thing you can't do is ignore them. Because they change things, they push the human race forward. And while some may see them as the crazy ones, we see genius. Because the people who are crazy enough to think they can change the world are the ones who do."- Rob Siltanen

FUN SHIT

Live - Laugh - Love.

PIECES OF AUSTRALIA (THROUGH MY EYES)

The list is at times long, all I can say is he was "A few stubbies short of a six- pack."

PIECES OF ME

Things you may know or may not know about me.

HISTORY

"Those who cannot remember the past are condemned to repeat it." – George Santayana, The Life of Reason (1905). From the series Great Ideas of Western Man. Which is EXACTLY what some historical accounts want.

MAKING MUSIC

Hell and Sunshine, that's how you taste - Tantalising.

POETRY

Poems by yours truly.

PROTEST

a statement or action expressing disapproval of or objection to something. "The team lodged an official protest".

TRUTH VS LIES

Be careful what lies you tell about me, some dick head's maybe corrected in

these books. Defamation is costly.

FREEMASONRY

"That a man be willing, when others are so too, as far forth as for peace and defense of himself he shall think it necessary, to lay down this right to all things; and be contented with so much liberty against other men, as he would allow other men against himself." - Thomas Hobbes

OPINIONS AND RANDOM SH*T

Opinions are like assholes, everyone's got one - these are mine. Plus, Anything but Ordinary random sh*t.

An individual is not subject to any civil, criminal or administrative liability for making a public interest disclosure. It is an offence to take a reprisal, or to threaten to take a reprisal, against a person because of a public interest disclosure (including a proposed or a suspected public interest disclosure). The Federal Court or Federal Circuit Court may make orders for civil remedies
(including compensation, injunctions, and reinstatement of employment) if a reprisal is taken against a person because of a public interest disclosure (including a proposed or a suspected public interest disclosure).
It is an offence to disclose the identity of an individual who makes a public interest disclosure.
Public Interest Disclosure Act 2013 No. 133, 2013

(Part 2; Subdivision A—Immunity from liability)

'Barbwire Noose', 'Fear Is The Root Of All Weakness', and the Barbwire logo are All Registered Trademarks.

www.ingramcontent.com/pod-product-compliance
Lightning Source LLC
Chambersburg PA
CBHW051313120626
46547CB00015B/2209